P9-CED-320

The
Resiliency
Advantage

also by Al Siebert:

The Adult Student's Guide to Survival and Success, (5th ed.),
  with Mary Karr, MS

*Gathering Wisdom: How to Acquire Wisdom from Others
  While Developing Your Own,* with Jerry Fletcher, Cheryl
  Matschek, MS, MH, and Gail Tycer, MS

The Resiliency Manual for Public Employees

*Student Success: How to Succeed in College and Still Have
  Time for Your Friends (8th ed.),* with Timothy L. Walter and
  Laurence Smith

*The Survivor Personality: Why Some People Are Stronger,
  Smarter, and More Skillful at Handling Life's Difficulties...
  and How You Can Be, Too*

The Resiliency Advantage

Master Change, Thrive Under Pressure, and Bounce Back from Setbacks

Al Siebert

BK

BERRETT-KOEHLER PUBLISHERS, INC.
San Francisco
a BK Life book

Copyright © 2005 by Al Siebert, PhD

All rights reserved. No part of this publication may be reproduced, distributed, or transmitted in any form or by any means, including photocopying, recording, or other electronic or mechanical methods, without the prior written permission of the publisher, except in the case of brief quotations embodied in critical reviews and certain other noncommercial uses permitted by copyright law. For permission requests, write to the publisher, addressed "Attention: Permissions Coordinator," at the address below.

Berrett-Koehler Publishers, Inc.
235 Montgomery Street, Suite 650
San Francisco, CA 94104-2916
Tel: (415) 288-0260   Fax: (415) 362-2512   www.bkconnection.com

Ordering Information
Quantity sales. Special discounts are available on quantity purchases by corporations, associations, and others. For details, contact the "Special Sales Department" at the Berrett-Koehler address above.
Individual sales. Berrett-Koehler publications are available through most bookstores. They can also be ordered directly from Berrett-Koehler:
Tel: (800) 929-2929; Fax: (802) 864-7626; www.bkconnection.com
Orders for college textbook/course adoption use. Please contact Berrett-Koehler: Tel: (800) 929-2929; Fax: (802) 864-7626.
Orders by U.S. trade bookstores and wholesalers. Please contact Ingram Publisher Services, Tel: (800) 509-4887; Fax: (800) 838-1149; E-mail: customer.service@ingrampublisherservices.com; or visit www.ingrampublisherservices.com/Ordering for details about electronic ordering.

Berrett-Koehler and the BK logo are registered trademarks of Berrett-Koehler Publishers, Inc.

Printed in the United States of America

Berrett-Koehler books are printed on long-lasting acid-free paper. When it is available, we choose paper that has been manufactured by environmentally responsible processes. These may include using trees grown in sustainable forests, incorporating recycled paper, minimizing chlorine in bleaching, or recycling the energy produced at the paper mill.

Library of Congress Cataloging-in-Publication Data

Siebert, Al.
   The resiliency advantage : master change, thrive under pressure and bounce back from setbacks / by Al Siebert.
      p. cm.
   Includes index.
   ISBN: 978-1-57675-329-3
   1. Resilience (Personality trait) I. Title
   BF698.35.R47S54 2005 155.2'4--dc22

                                        2004062331

FIRST EDITION
15 14 13   10 9 8

Text/illustration design by Kristin Pintarich, www.kpservices.us
Cover design by Leslie Waltzer, www.crowfootdesign.com

Contents

Preface

A Head Start on Resiliency

Have you ever been some place and sensed that something wasn't quite right? I felt that way when I was close to completing my graduate program in clinical psychology. I had a nagging feeling that something was off, but couldn't quite grasp what it was.

Then the answer came to me—like in a cartoon when a light bulb turns on over someone's head. I'd been told over and over that I was going into the mental health profession, but I'd never been given any classes on mental health. I suddenly realized that clinical psychology and psychiatry were not mental health professions; they were mental illness professions.[1]

I saw, for example, that the National Institute of Mental Health had no information available about mental health, indicators of mental health, or how to develop mental health. The entire focus of the NIMH was (and still is) to research causes and treatments of mental illnesses.[2]

To help overcome this deficit in my education, I gave the students in a course I was teaching a special term-paper assignment. They had to describe "A Psychologically Healthy Person."

Reading term papers written by thirty psychology majors gave me an overview of what was known at the time, but mostly their papers showed that the field of psychology contained little knowledge about individuals with excellent mental health. The standard view was that mental health is assumed to exist in people without symptoms of mental illness.

After I graduated, I started a personal research project to

understand people so mentally healthy they can survive extreme life adversities without becoming psychological casualties, and emerge stronger than before. I thought back to the combat survivors I'd served with in the paratroopers after the Korean War. During my three years with them, I saw that it wasn't luck or chance that they were the few that came back alive. Something about them as people had tipped the scales in their favor.

I remembered being fascinated with Dr. Viktor Frankl, when he came to my college to speak about his experiences in the Nazi death camps during the Holocaust. He was not bitter or angry; he was a happy man.

I become intrigued with what Abraham Maslow called a "continental divide" principle. "I use this principle," he wrote, "to describe the fact that stress will break people altogether if they are in the beginning too weak to stand distress, or else, if they are already strong enough to take the stress in the first place, that same stress, if they come through it, will strengthen them, temper them, and make them stronger."[3]

I wondered, "Why do some people emerge from extreme difficulties stronger and better than before? How do they do that?"

I read books by survivors and interviewed hundreds of people willing to talk about their survival experiences. I explored survivor resiliency at depths never taught in any psychology courses. Instead of using traditional research methods, I asked questions and listened until a consistent pattern took form. I explored the territory until a map revealed itself to me. After many years of listening and learning, I developed a good understanding of what I call "the survivor personality."

My findings about life's best survivors were published in *The Survivor Personality* in 1996. When it came out, I received requests from many corporations, professional associations, education and healthcare groups wanting to know how to use the survivor personality traits to cope with workplace challenges. Almost half the requests came from public-sector groups struggling to sustain essential services after layoffs and budget reductions.

Ten years of teaching and speaking about how to be resilient led to this book. *The Resiliency Advantage* picks up where *The Survivor Personality* left off. This book is unique in many ways:

+ Most books by psychologists and psychiatrists with "resiliency" titles are recovery books written for emotionally traumatized people wanting to live normal lives. In contrast, *The Resiliency Advantage* shows basically healthy people how to become better and better at handling turbulent change, nonstop pressure, and life-disrupting setbacks.

+ It is written more like an owner's manual than a self-help book. It explains how you can access and benefit from many inborn abilities that few people use very well. It describes principles and processes that lead to becoming resilient, and provides resiliency development guidelines showing how to apply the information in your circumstances as you think best.

+ It is the first book to describe the different levels of resiliency that people achieve. Just as students in martial arts must learn basic skills before they can acquire higher levels of skill, this book shows how certain basic resiliency skills provide the foundation for mastering higher-level abilities.

+ It is the first job-related, coping-skills book to include challenges faced by public-sector employees. *The Resiliency Advantage* recognizes that people who work in the public sector need and appreciate useful resiliency guidelines as much as those who work in the private sector or are self-employed.

+ This book is also an invitation to participate in a breakthrough journey of discovery. Chapter 13 lists many indicators that we humans are transforming to a different way of being human. As you develop your resiliency strengths, you will find that you can handle a world of constant, disruptive change easily and naturally.

These are challenging times. We are in a turbulent era. One in which too much change is happening too fast for many people. *The Resiliency Advantage* gives you a head start over those who don't want to learn skills for handling constant change and difficult developments. This book shows you how to sustain strong, healthy energy in non-stop change, bounce back quickly from setbacks, and gain strength from adversities.

Al Siebert, PhD, Director
The Resiliency Center
Portland, Oregon
March, 2005

Chapter One

Thriving in Today's World

Cynthia Dailey-Hewkin poured herself a hot cup of coffee, sat down at the little table in her kitchen, and opened the morning paper. Her eyes widened, her jaw dropped open when she saw the front-page headline announcing that the Trojan nuclear plant where she worked was going to shut down. She was shocked. Her first thought was, "Oh no! What am I going to do?"

Cynthia says, "The plant closure came at a particularly difficult time in my life. I was going through a divorce after being married twenty-eight years, and my mother was dying of a brain tumor. Now I was losing my job."[1]

* * * * * * * * * * * * * *

How do you respond to extreme setbacks? People react to life's rough blows in many different ways. Some emotionally explode. They become enraged and flail around. They have emotional tantrums in which they may want to hurt someone. A few become physically violent.

Others do the opposite. They implode. They go numb. They feel so helpless and overwhelmed they can't even try to cope with what has happened.

Some people portray themselves as victims. They blame others for ruining their lives. They spiral downward, mired in unhappy thoughts and feelings. "This isn't fair," they complain over and over. "Look at what they've done to me now."

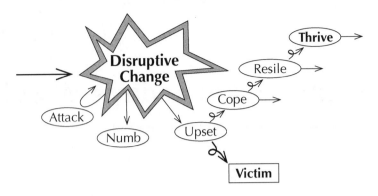

© 1993, 1996 Al Siebert

Then, as shown above, there is another group, the people who get through their distress, orient quickly to the new reality, and cope with immediate challenges. They bounce back and often spiral upward, stronger and better than before. In the workplace, they convert what could be a major career loss into finding an even better new career.

Highly resilient people are flexible, adapt to new circumstances quickly, and thrive in constant change. Most importantly, they *expect* to bounce back and feel confident they will. They have a knack for creating good luck out of circumstances that many others see as bad luck.

In the past, individuals had to learn how to become resilient on their own. Now, for the first time, the new science of resiliency psychology can show you how to become quickly and easily resilient in a way that fits your world. Research into coping, optimism, hardiness, stress-resistance, post-traumatic growth, creativity, emotional intelligence, and the survivor personality has identified the main attributes of resiliency. In the chapters ahead, you will learn how to use knowledge gained from the latest psychology research to develop your unique way of being resilient.

Avoiding the Victim Reaction

Sadly, some people get stuck in the victim/blaming mode when their lives are disrupted. They reject all suggestions on how to cope with what happened. They won't take steps to overcome their difficulties even after the crisis is over. Getting stuck in this frame of mind is like tying a rope around your feet and then trying to run a race—it's a major handicap. Victim thinking keeps people feeling helpless, and by blaming others for their bad situations, they place responsibility on others for making their lives better.

"Reaction" is used here in the sense of a reflex that happens without any conscious thought or feeling of choices. "Response" indicates that your actions after a threat or setback are guided by conscious choices.

Blaming others for ruining the life you had will block you from bouncing back. Blaming an organization's executives, "the government," self-serving politicians, administrators who lack emotional intelligence, cheap foreign labor, stock market managers, taxpayers, or any person or group for ruining your life keeps you in a non-resilient victim state in which you do not take resiliency actions.

Your opinion is probably right, of course. As corporate consultant Gary Hamel has observed, "The world is becoming turbulent faster than organizations are becoming resilient."[2] The chaos of change in today's world is beyond the ability of most organizations to handle well. Some executives and administrators manage their organizations in ways that hamper employee resiliency. Changes in the workplace occur so often now that very few employees have up-to-date job descriptions. And it isn't just frequent, disruptive change that must be handled. Morale suffers when friendships with co-workers are disrupted by reorganization, downsizing, and layoffs. Pride in one's work can be hard to maintain when a system you developed for doing things is tossed out and a new system that doesn't work as well is imposed on you.

When groups of employees make lists of their challenges and difficulties, they often tell me that there may be an impressive mission statement posted in the front lobby, but back where they work, they feel pressured to do more work of better quality in less time, with fewer people, in new ways, using new technology and new methods on a reduced budget—while worrying if their jobs are safe. An older manager in a large retail store said, "It used to be that when you took on a bigger workload, worked through your lunch hour, and took work home, you were trying to get a promotion. Now it means you may be able to keep your job three months longer."

The shock of an unexpected layoff can be devastating to someone who has enjoyed strong career progress and expects even more career success. Some people feel crushed and remain depressed for a long time. Some may settle for much lower paying jobs and drift into bitterness about how they feel mistreated. A former manager of a manufacturing plant kept telling upper level executives that they shouldn't change anything in "his" plant because everything was working fine and his operation was profitable. When they fired him because he refused to consider making changes they wanted, he did not cope well. Three years later, he still felt angry and bitter as he worked to support his family by driving a taxicab in Chicago—an occupation he felt was beneath him.

Negative emotions such as fear, anger, anxiety, distress, helplessness, and hopelessness decrease your ability to solve the problems you face, and they weaken your resiliency. Constant fears and worries weaken your immune system and increase your vulnerability to illnesses. Taking tranquilizers is not a good long-term solution; neither is using alcohol to sleep at night and stimulants to become energized in the morning.

The situation is serious. At the present time, one out of six Americans uses tranquilizers regularly. According to current US Food and Drug Administration figures, approximately 1.5 million adults are tranquilizer addicts, and tranquilizer misusers currently outnumber abusers of illicit drugs.[3]

A significant benefit from developing resiliency strengths is that you cope so well that you are less likely to need tranquilizers. If the organization you work for is unstable because the executives and administrators can't manage rapid change, it's possible to find ways to handle the pressure and keep bouncing back without anxiety attacks.

The Resiliency Response—Not Easy, But Worth the Effort

Resiliency means being able to bounce back from life developments that may feel totally overwhelming at first. When resilient people have their lives disrupted they handle their feelings in healthy ways. They allow themselves to feel grief, anger, loss, and confusion when hurt and distressed, but they don't let it become a permanent feeling state. An unexpected outcome is that they not only heal, they often bounce back stronger than before. They are examples of Wilhelm Nietzsche's famous statement, "That which does not kill me makes me stronger."[4]

This is why resilient people usually handle major difficulties easier than others. They expect to rebuild their disrupted lives in a new way that works for them, and the struggle to overcome adversity develops new strengths in them.

Definitions:

Resilience, resilient, and *resiliency* refer to the ability to
  ▶ cope well with high levels of ongoing disruptive change;
  ▶ sustain good health and energy when under constant pressure;
  ▶ bounce back easily from setbacks;
  ▶ overcome adversities;
  ▶ change to a new way of working and living when an old way is no longer possible; and
  ▶ do all this without acting in dysfunctional or harmful ways.

If you look in an unabridged dictionary, you will see that "resile" is the verb for resilience and "resiling" is the adverb. The words "resile" and "resiling" will be used in this book at times to emphasize that resiliency is something you *do*, more than something you *have*.

Resilience is more important than ever in today's world. The volatile and chaotic period we are going through will not end soon. To sustain a good life for yourself and your family, you must be much more resilient than people had to be in the past. People with resiliency skills have a significant advantage over those who feel helpless or react like victims. In this world of life-disrupting, nonstop change

- Corporations with highly resilient employees have an advantage over their less resilient competitors.
- During downsizing, a resilient worker with a wide range of skills has better chance of being kept on.
- When many people are applying for one job, a resilient person has a better chance of being hired.
- When your old job skills are no longer needed, you are quick to learn a new way to earn an income.
- During economic hardship, resilient people give their families a better chance of pulling through and bouncing back.
- Resilient people help their communities get through hard times better.
- Resiliency is crucial when there are the added challenges of physical injury or living through a terrorist attack.
- A resilient person is best at making difficult situations work well.
- Resilient people are less likely to become ill during difficult times.

Resiliency is an essential skill in every job sector—in corporations, small businesses, public agencies, professional services, and the self-employed—especially during times of turmoil. It is important to understand that when you are hit with life-disrupting events, you will never be the same again. You either cope or you crumble; you become better or bitter; you emerge stronger or weaker.

* * * * * * * * * * * * * *

Cynthia Dailey-Hewkin sat and stared out her kitchen window as she absorbed the shock of learning about the closure of the nuclear plant where she worked. "I'd left a difficult, twenty-eight-year marriage," she says, "to set out on my own with little money. I'd moved out of a nice home into a low-rent apartment that I hated. I'd been through weeks of my mother dying. All things considered, when I compared losing my job to everything else I'd been through, it wasn't the worst. It was one more challenge I had to add to my list."

At the plant, her co-workers expressed anguish, anger, dismay, and many other feelings. Cynthia listened to them and occasionally offered suggestions on how to cope.

Cynthia avoided self-pity. She thought back to some wise counseling she had received from a chaplain when she had sought help about her troubled marriage. "The chaplain told me to list six things I can do, then pick one and do it." Now she asked herself, "What can I do?" She outlined a plan to cope with her income loss and listed steps she would take to search for a new job. "I never felt like a victim," she said, "and never blamed anyone. I told myself, 'This is just life.'"

The closing of the nuclear plant and the related layoffs occurred in phases extending many months. Cynthia was told she had about eight months before her job would end. She felt compassion for her co-workers worried about future financial difficulties. She asked herself, "What can I do to help?"

"I like to write," she said, "so I contacted the editor of the Trojan Plant newsletter and offered to write a column with money-saving hints. He was enthusiastic. He gave me my own column, 'Saving with Cynthia.' Kind of corny, but it had a nice big heading! People reading it were most appreciative." Cynthia found herself doing informal career counseling. "I found I had a knack for helping people identify their best skills and find new jobs."

Cynthia applied for jobs, but without success. She remembers that "it felt scary. We were competing against our co-workers for every job opening announced by Portland General Electric, the parent company. Interviews were often held at the plant, and sometimes there would be lines of people applying for the same job."

Meanwhile, her helpfulness to her co-workers and "can-do" spirit impressed the managers in the human resources department at PGE's corporate headquarters. She said, "They called me and said they wanted me to work in HR! I felt elated! I started my new HR job on the Monday after my job at the Trojan plant ended. I didn't lose one day of work or any benefits, and they paid me more than I'd been earning at Trojan. Things worked out much better than I'd imagined."

Cynthia remarried several years later and moved with her husband to another city. Her career changes have continued. Today she has her "dream job," working as an employment specialist in a college career center offering free services to the unemployed. She says, "If it weren't for the layoff at Trojan, none of this would have happened! It helped open the doors for me to a whole new world."

• • • • • • • • • • • • • • •

Notice that Cynthia said she never let herself feel like a victim. Her reaction was to focus on handling the many challenges and help her co-workers as well. She dealt with her situation in her way, and the outcome was even better than she dreamed possible.

Learning to Be Resilient

In the past, individuals had to find ways to be resilient on their own. Now, however, the emerging new science of resiliency psychology has identified what strengths to acquire and how almost anyone can develop them. The resiliency guidelines in this book focus mainly on resiliency in the workplace, but they apply broadly to all aspects of life. By developing resiliency skills and strengths where you work, you then have those same skills available if hit by difficult or trying circumstances in any other area of your life. The most empowering finding in resiliency-psychology research is that you have an inborn predisposition to become resilient and change-proficient. The personal resiliency plan in this book shows you how to

- ✦ remain calm under pressure, bounce back from setbacks, and avoid resiliency fatigue;
- ✦ improve your problem-solving skills by using three different methods: analytical, creative, and practical;
- ✦ keep a playful sense of humor, optimism, and positive feelings during rough times;
- ✦ break free from inner barriers to resiliency by strengthen-

ing your inner "selfs" in healthy ways and overcoming the "good child" handicap;

+ overcome tendencies to feel like a victim, and stay detached from "victim" reactions in others;
+ value your complex qualities such as selfish unselfishness, optimistic pessimism, and cooperative nonconformity;
+ develop your unique way of being resilient by being both self-reliant and socially responsible;
+ discover how your natural desire to learn is what leads to your life getting better and better;
+ become skillful at having things work well for you and others;
+ convert misfortune into good fortune; and
+ master the art of resiliency.

This book will not tell you what to do or how to act or think. You've had too much of that in your life. People *trained* to think, feel, and perform as instructed may be prepared for expected difficulties, but not for unexpected or unique difficulties. "Trained" people fear change and don't problem solve quickly in unexpected circumstances, not in the way that resilient people do. Resilient people are those who consciously decide that somehow, some way, they will do the very best they can to survive, cope, and make things turn out well.

Your resiliency strengths come from self-motivated, self-managed efforts to develop resiliency skills. Some people who hear or read about ways to become more resilient mistakenly think that the power lies in the recommended method. They go through the steps in a detached way thinking that the technique will make things better. Then when things don't turn out well, they blame the technique for not working. This is like tossing a can opener at a can of food and then blaming the can opener when the can doesn't open.

While writing this book, I received an e-mail from a man feeling distressed and angry about losing his job. At the end of my reply to him, I sent him a link to my website article, "Guidelines for Handling the Emotional Side of Job Loss and Job Search."

He responded immediately, "I DID THAT CRAP. IT DID NOT GET ME ANYWHERE!"[5]

Just as a can opener doesn't open cans by itself, reading about resiliency skills doesn't make a person resilient. Resiliency comes from deciding to learn good skills for bouncing back from setbacks and working to have things turn out well. Your intention to develop resiliency methods that work for you is what determines your success or failure.

The Five Levels of Resiliency and Three Barriers to Overcome

A few people are born resilient. Like natural athletes, they have it in them from the start. The rest of us have inborn resiliency potentials that we can access and develop if we choose to. You were born with the ability to learn how to hold up under pressure, adapt quickly to change, bounce back from setbacks, and find ways to have bad situations to turn out well.

Chapter 3 emphasizes the importance of deciding to control much of what is happening in your life, and it lists eight principles and beliefs affecting resiliency. One important principle, true for anyone motivated to increase his or her resiliency, is to understand that we humans can learn new abilities at any age. Developing your resiliency strengths, however, may require overcoming and breaking free from three barriers to resiliency that handicap people who

- were raised to be a "good" boy or girl;
- are overly socialized to conform and believe that external forces control your life; and
- believe the social myth of "stress."

In the chapters ahead you will learn how to free yourself from these three barriers to resiliency.

The steps for developing your resiliency skills and strengths follow a hierarchy of five levels. Each one builds on the one before. These are to accomplish the following:

1. Optimize your health and well-being
2. Develop good problem-solving skills

3. Develop strong inner gatekeepers
4. Develop high-level resiliency skills
5. Discover your talent for serendipity

The first level shows how to create and follow a personal plan for optimizing your health and energy using a simple, practical action plan. In chapter 4, you will learn ways to use what is known about emotional and physical mind-body connections to free yourself from myths about stress. Level One skills include handling your feelings in emotionally competent ways during times of too much change and too many pressures. This well-tested, practical, realistic plan is flexible so that you can adapt it to your unique nature. Psychologists know, for example, that a quiet person needs time alone to recover from distress, while an outgoing person needs to talk with others.

The second level prepares you to focus outward to problem solve challenges. Psychology research shows that problem-focused responses to unexpected difficulties lead to resiliency, while strong emotional reactions in which you feel like a victim lead to helplessness. In chapter 5, you will learn how to strengthen your problem-solving skills using three kinds of human intelligence: analytical, creative, and practical.

The third level focuses inward on three mind-body dimensions that determine resiliency—strong self-esteem, self-confidence, and a positive self-concept based on moral values. Chapter 6 explains how these three core "selfs" function like gatekeepers to your higher-level abilities. If they are weak, you will not be very resilient. If they are strong and healthy, you can access and develop many resiliency strengths.

Resiliency research shows that the biggest barrier to resiliency for some people is their "good child" upbringing. As you will see in chapters 6 and 7, having been raised to be a good boy or girl can prevent you from doing what it takes to be resilient when your world is shaken up. In your personal resiliency plan, you will learn how to overcome inner barriers to resiliency by developing and strengthening the three gatekeepers to an optimal level.

At *the fourth level* you develop abilities and skills found in highly resilient people. Chapter 7 shows how childlike curiosity and self-managed learning lead to advanced resiliency skills.

Our ancestors knew about the power of hope. Chapter 8 provides new information about optimism, positive thinking, coping skills, and resiliency that can empower you during times of adversity.

Chapter 9 is a stretch for many people. It explains how to gain deep mental and emotional stability by developing a flexibly complex, unique personality. The most resilient people reach a level of development where they gain strength from counterbalanced inner qualities. They are not socially compliant, for example, but act in socially responsible ways.

In chapter 10, you will see that the best way to understand highly resilient people is to observe what happens around them. In a workplace without up-to-date job descriptions, they are more effective than others because they are free to interact with the moment-to-moment action in ways that lead to things working well for everyone. They work less hard than others, however, because they have mastered the art of allowing things to work well.

The fifth level is the highest level of resiliency. People at this level have a major advantage in a world of constant change. They don't fight against disruptive change because they accept new realities quickly. They know that everything in the world happens the way it should. They align rapidly to new realities and allow themselves to influence events so that things turn out well. As shown in chapter 11, highly resilient people can dance and flow with disruptive change because they have many attitudes and perspectives that let them be both involved and detached from the action. Resiliency lets you align quickly to new circumstances and steer the swirling energies to reach good outcomes. A reliable strength at this level is the talent for serendipity—the ability to convert accidents and misfortune into lucky accidents and good fortune.

Stories of survivors of extreme resiliency challenges can be inspiring. Chapter 12 describes how some people not only survive circumstances that overwhelm others, they recover stronger and better. Lance Armstrong, for example, almost died from cancer that had spread to many organs in his body. He had extensive surgery, underwent chemotherapy, survived the cancer, and came back to win the Tour de France bicycle race, year after year. In interviews Armstrong has said, "If I had to choose between getting testicular cancer and winning the Tour de France, I would choose testicular cancer." He describes his bout with cancer as "a special wake-up call." The cancer left him scarred physically and emotionally. "But it was an unexpected gift." He says his recovery ordeal changed him. It awakened him to fully appreciate the blessings of good health, a loving family, and close friends.[6]

. . . .

Three elements lead to personal effectiveness—you know *what* has to be done, know *how* to do it, and feel *motivated* to do it. At the end of each chapter, you will find suggested Resiliency Development Activities. You will increase the speed and depth of your resiliency development by doing the activities, recording what you learn in a private journal, and discussing what you are learning with others.

The five levels of resiliency described in this book provide you with a comprehensive, personalized system for bouncing back faster and easier and living a longer, healthier, more enjoyable life. This program shows how to use knowledge from the new *science* of resiliency psychology to learn the art of resiliency. It shows how to benefit from aligning your mind, attitudes, and actions with the reality that our world is a vibrant, dynamic place of unceasing change.

A significant benefit from being self-confident, change-proficient, optimistic, and skilled at making things work well is that you master the process of nonstop change. As described in chapter 13, the pressures of nonstop, disruptive change appear to be motivating a human transformation to a new way of being. Your ability to resile over and over comes from allowing your mind, attitudes, feelings, values, skills, and unique nature to be different in every situation, organized by your purposeful consciousness.

The art of resiliency gives you a powerful advantage in today's world. Your learning will be most useful if you put together your own plan for developing your way of being resilient and don't restrict yourself only to what you read in this book. In the school of life, the responsibility is on the learner, not the teacher.

Before reading further about resiliency, take the resiliency self-assessment, "How Resilient Are You?" in chapter 2. It will give you an overview of the most important resiliency skills and indicate how well you use them now.

Resiliency Development Activities

1. What differences have you noticed between people who are highly resilient and those who are not very resilient? Make two lists.

2. Something done with great skill may be described as "an art." Dozens of books have been written on topics such as *The Art of Happiness, The Art of Leadership, The Art of Conversation, The Art of War,* and so forth. What does doing anything as "an art" mean to you? What are your thoughts about "the art of resiliency?" What appeals to you about learning resiliency as "an art?"

3. The chapters ahead have embedded within them an unstated, essential resiliency skill. See if you can identify what it is.

Chapter Two

How Resilient Are You?

My thirty years of self-funded research to understand highly resilient survivors once got me a free lunch. The invitation came from Carol Angel, a certified public accountant (CPA) who specialized in small businesses. Carol said she had attended a leadership workshop I conducted for her state CPA society a few years before on the nature of life's best survivors. "This lunch is my way of thanking you," she said, "for making my business so successful."

"Thank you," I said, "but how did I do that?"

She explained. "After hearing you speak I decided I would only accept clients who matched your description of the survivor personality. Whenever someone with a small business asks me to become their accountant, I tell them I want to become acquainted with them first. Mixed in with many questions about their business and business experience, I ask questions from your list. I accept as clients only the ones who match your description—about one out of three."

Smiling broadly, she said, "You probably know that the survival rate for people starting small businesses is low. But most of my clients succeed. I don't have the same problems that most CPAs do with clients going through bankruptcy, owing back taxes, missing payrolls, having liens against their assets, and being hounded by collection agencies. Thank you very, very much!"

I thanked her, and then pointed out that she was showing

many of the traits found in resilient survivors. She related to resiliency qualities in her clients because she had them herself.

● ● ● ● ● ● ● ● ● ● ● ● ● ● ●

Resiliency-psychology research has identified why some people are more resilient than others. The self-assessment that follows covers the key abilities, attitudes, and attributes found in highly resilient people. It will help you identify areas where you are strong and areas that need to be strengthened. It can also serve as a way to identify highly resilient people when that is important to you.

Resiliency Quiz

Rate yourself on the following items:

(1 = very little, 5 = very strong)

___ In a crisis or chaotic situation, I calm myself and focus on taking useful actions.

___ I'm usually optimistic. I see difficulties as temporary, expect to overcome them, and believe things will turn out well.

___ I can tolerate high levels of uncertainty and ambiguity.

___ I adapt quickly to new developments. I'm good at bouncing back from difficulties.

___ I'm playful. I find the humor in rough situations, laugh at myself, and am easily amused.

___ I'm able to recover emotionally from losses and setbacks. I have friends I can talk with. I can express my feelings to others and can ask for help.

___ I feel self-confident, appreciate myself, and have a healthy concept of who I am.

___ I'm curious. I ask questions. I want to know how things work. I like to try new ways of doing things.

___ I learn valuable lessons from my experiences and from the experiences of others.

___ I'm good at solving problems. I can think in analytical, creative, or practical ways.

___ I'm good at making things work well. I'm often asked to lead groups and projects.

___ I'm very flexible. I feel comfortable with my paradoxical complexity. I'm optimistic and pessimistic, trusting and cautious, unselfish and selfish, and so forth.

___ I'm always myself, but I've noticed that I'm different with different people and in different situations.

___ I prefer to work without a written job description. I'm more effective when I'm free to do what I think is best in each situation.

___ I "read" people well and trust my intuition.

___ I'm a good listener, I have good empathy skills.

___ I'm nonjudgmental about others and am comfortable with many kinds of people.

___ I'm very durable. I hold up well during tough times. I have an independent spirit underneath my cooperative way of working with others.

___ I've been made stronger and better by difficult experiences.

___ I've converted misfortune into good luck and found benefits in bad experiences.

Total points: _____

Scoring:

Low score: A self-rating score under 50 indicates that life is a probably a struggle for you and you know it. You may not handle pressure well. You don't learn anything useful from bad experiences. You feel hurt when people criticize you. You may sometimes feel helpless and without hope.

If these statements fit you, ask yourself, "Would I like to learn how to handle my difficulties better?" If your answer is yes, then a good way to start is to meet with others who are working to develop their resiliency skills. Let them coach, encourage, and guide you. Another way, if you work for a large employer, is to get resiliency coaching from a counselor with the Employee Assistance Program. The fact that you feel motivated to be more resilient is a positive sign.

High score: If you rated yourself high on most of these statements, you have a score over 90. This means you know you're already very good at bouncing back from life's set-backs. For you, this book will validate many things you are doing right. And, because you like learning new ways to be even better, it will show you how to take your already good skills to a very high level—something like reaching an advanced-degree black-belt level in the martial arts.

A question for you to consider is how much you feel willing to tell your story to others and make yourself available to people who are trying to cope with adversities. People learn from real-life role models. You could be one.

Middle scores: If you agreed with many of the statements and scored in the 70–89 range, then that is very good! It means you will gain a lot from this book and will become even more self-confident and resilient than before. You will become better and better at bouncing back from adversities.

If you scored in the 50–69 range, you appear to be fairly adequate, but you may be underrating yourself. A much larger percentage of people underrate themselves than over-rate themselves on the assessment. Some people have a habit of being modest and automatically give themselves a 3 on every item for a total score of 60. If your score is in the 50–69 range, we need to find out how valid your self-rating is.

One validity check is to ask two people who know you well to rate you on the items and see what scores they come up with. Have a discussion with them about of each of the items where there is a discrepancy and listen to what they say. If they rate you higher, this may indicate that you had a "good child" upbringing that is keeping you from being as resilient as you could be.

A second way of checking the validity of your self-rating is to answer these bonus point questions:

+ Has your sense of humor ever gotten you into trouble?

+ Has asking questions ever gotten you into trouble?

+ Has being unpredictable or too complex ever puzzled or bothered others?

+ Has your effort to anticipate problems ever had someone accuse you of having a negative attitude?

+ Are you such a good listener your ability to understand both sides of a conflict has confused others?

Give yourself a point for every yes to the bonus point questions above, plus an additional bonus point for the item in the quiz regarding self-confidence and self-esteem. These extra questions help show that you may not see the connection between some of what you do and resiliency. The chapters and activities ahead will reveal more resiliency abilities in you than you ever thought were possible. The next chapter shows how adversity brought out strengths in people who didn't know how resilient they could be.

Chapter Three

Bouncing Back from Setbacks

- - - - - - - - - - - - - -

What do you do when your life is shattered? What do you do when the bright future you expected for yourself feels like it is collapsing into ruins? People who have bounced back from devastating setbacks are inspiring, real-life examples of resiliency.

• • • • • • • • • • • • • •

Gert Lamfrom and Neal Boyle were college sweethearts. After they married, Neal began working in her parent's small hat-manufacturing business. He learned the business well and eventually took over as its president.

In 1970, Neal died suddenly of a heart attack. Gert's grief was magnified by seeing that no one but her husband knew how to run the business, and her parents were too old to come back. All their assets were in the business. If it collapsed, she didn't know what she could do to support herself, her parents, and her son in college.

Gert decided she would do her best not to let their small business collapse. She asked her son Tim, a senior in college, to come home and help her save the company from bankruptcy. With debts mounting and workers to pay, they worked long days and on weekends to fill and ship orders.

The business stabilized and they decided to expand by making sportswear. Gert was ruthless in making certain every item was perfect before it shipped. The company, Columbia Sportswear, developed strong brand awareness in 1984 when it launched an advertising campaign that featured Gert as a stern taskmaster with incredibly high standards. The ads featured "Mother Boyle" peering over her glasses, admonishing son Tim to ruthlessly test the durability of Columbia Sportswear garments.

Under Gert's leadership, Columbia Sportswear did more than bounce back from near collapse. Over the years it grew from being a small hat-manufacturing company to become one of the world's largest producers of sportswear, outdoor clothing, and ski wear.[1]

Who Is Responsible?

For many decades, our society trained children to be controlled by authorities. This benefits people in positions of authority but can prevent many adults from being resilient when their well-being is determined by their responses to unexpected difficulties. In the past, most private-sector and public-sector employees were hired and retained because they were easily controlled. Their upbringing oversocialized them into acquiescing to people in authority. The unwritten agreement was that if they cooperated, did as told, and didn't cause problems when feeling upset with management, they would have a lifetime job with fringe benefits and a good retirement package. The arrangement worked reasonably well for most employees while it lasted, but that world doesn't exist anymore. It is now common to hear about excellent employees losing their jobs because of organizational downsizing.

When your life is disrupted by decisions or actions made by others, an essential question to ask yourself is, "Who is responsible for how well my life goes?" How resilient you are depends on your answer. Here's why:

During the 1960s, Julian Rotter (rhymes with "motor") developed a psychological test that could predict which students at his university were likely to initiate action to protest against the Vietnam war, and which ones would not take action unless led. Rotter's research found that those most likely to take self-motivated action felt that primary control of their lives was inside themselves. He described them as having an "internal locus of control." Those who felt that the primary point of control in their lives was outside themselves seldom initiated action to make changes, no matter how unhappy they felt about their problems. Rotter described them as having an "external locus of control."

A paradoxical finding in the external/internal-control research is that *both sets of beliefs are self-validating and self-fulfilling.* People who believe that their fate is under the control of outside forces act in ways that confirm their beliefs. People who know they can do things to make life better act in ways that confirm their beliefs.[3]

Here's a quiz to show you the differences between internal and external feelings of control. Which one of the following statements in each pair do you believe is more true than the other?

Pick choice *a* or choice *b*.

1a. The events that affect my life are beyond my control.
1b. I feel responsible for how well my life goes.

2a. Having a good marriage means you were lucky to find the right person.
2b. A good marriage comes from both partners working at it.

3a. Employees will slack off if a strong boss doesn't tell them what to do.
3b. Employees work best when they are given clear goals and freedom to work in their own way.

4a. Promotions usually come from being liked by the right people.
4b. Promotions are usually earned through hard work and persistence.

5a. Making a lot of money comes from getting the right breaks.
5b. A person's income is determined mostly by ability.

6a. Luck determines success or failure in life.
6b. Good planning and hard work determine success in life.

7a. I would be happier if the politicians and business leaders did their jobs better.

7b. It is possible to have a happy life even when there are many social and economic problems.

8a. Some people are easy to get along with and others aren't.

8b. Good relationships with others is a skill that can be learned.

9a. If your life is tough, that's your bad luck.

9b. Life isn't fair, but I usually learn good lessons from bad experiences.

10a. People can't change what they are like.

10b. People can learn better ways to do things if they try.

Scoring:
The first statement in each pair reflects external control beliefs. The *a* choices reflect a belief that outside forces, luck, and chance determine how a person's life goes. The second statement in each pair reflects internal control beliefs. The *b* statements reflect the belief that you are able to learn from experience and influence how well your life goes.[2]

Hundreds of research studies show that people who cope best in difficult situations score high on measures of "internal control" beliefs. They feel personally responsible for how well their lives go, and know that they have some control over events and their responses to events.

People who feel helpless and victimized, and blame others, score high on measures of "external control" beliefs. They do not believe that their personal efforts could make anything better. They believe that solutions to their unhappy condition are under the control of other people and external forces. If you identify with internal control beliefs, it may be hard to accept that many people choose the first answer in the assessment. That's why they never take action when you suggest a way for them to handle something better. I run into this all the time in my workshops. A common question is, "How can I get my co-worker to stop complaining all the time?" If I suggest several ways to be less vulnerable to the complaining, I often hear that the person asking the question wants others to change. They don't want suggestions on how they might change their own responses. Or they shrug and say, "What good would it do anyway?"

Resilient people don't wait for others to rescue them; they work through their feelings, set goals, work to reach their goals, and often emerge from the resiliency process with a better life than before. Later, they say they are glad that their difficult situation happened.

From Disaster to Breakthrough

In many ways, being resilient is more essential to the survival and success of small business owners than good business practices or technical knowledge. Small business owners are vulnerable to many problems and setbacks that can put them out of business. That's why very few small businesses last and are profitable five years after starting.

An effort to be resilient instead of being crushed by major adversity may require small business owners to learn new areas of expertise and do things never expected in their original plans. The resiliency response may not be quick. It can take a long time—and it can lead to a business growing far beyond what was imagined in the beginning.

● ● ● ● ● ● ● ● ● ● ● ● ● ●

While attending college as a music major, Bill Harris became fascinated with the positive mental and emotional effects that came from listening to combinations of pure sound waves on stereo headphones. After much experimenting, he created sophisticated audio recordings that put people quickly into the same deep meditational state that some people achieve only after years of practice. Listening to his stereo recordings led to accelerated learning, enhanced creativity, clarity of consciousness, and even increased spirituality.

In 1989, Bill and one of his friends started a small, part-time business to market their specialized recordings. They named the company Centerpointe Research Institute because most of their users reported feeling more centered after listening to the recordings. The company's first year wasn't very successful, however; they had only forty-three customers and little profit.

Then something happened that seemed disastrous to their business. Bill was served with papers notifying him that a competitor had filed a one-million-dollar lawsuit accusing Bill and his partner of stealing the competitor's audio technology, customer list, and more.

Bill says, "My stomach turned as I envisioned losing my house and everything I owned, even though I knew the accusations were false and the lawsuit entirely frivolous. I asked my attorney what the legal fees were likely to be as the lawsuit proceeded. He said if the suit went all the way to trial, the legal fees could total $150,000 or more. At the time, I had perhaps $5,000, so this huge number was quite a shock. My business partner, who was equally panicked, thought we should just fold up and move on to something else.

"But I didn't agree. I was enjoying what I was doing—really for the first time in my life—and was actually beginning to get some recognition as an expert. What's more, I felt considerable resistance to the idea of allowing myself to be driven out of business by a bully who had filed a frivolous lawsuit in an attempt to eliminate a better product from competition.

"Over the next few months, I had many middle-of-the-night anxiety attacks where I would suddenly sit up in bed with a pounding heart as I contemplated the worst. My tapes helped me relax, and even though I had spells of feeling intensely afraid, fear and anxiety weren't my only reactions. I'd been reading Napoleon Hill's famous book, *Think and Grow Rich*, in which Hill says, 'Every adversity carries with it the seed of an equivalent or greater benefit.' To experience this benefit, however, you must look for it and germinate it. I forced myself to sit at my desk and, with a shaking hand, begin to make a list of the 'potential benefits' of being sued for a million dollars.

"At first, Hill's idea seemed ridiculous. What could possibly be beneficial about being sued for a million dollars? As I started my feeble list, the first few benefits didn't seem very significant. The first was 'I'll learn a lot about the legal system'—a benefit I would have certainly been willing to forego. However, over a few weeks, I thought of several others, and the list ultimately grew to contain over sixty benefits—every one of which ultimately came true.

"Here's how the biggest of these benefits came true. I did something that absolutely changed my life and brought me the most significant of all the 'seeds of an equivalent or greater benefit' I had listed. I wish I could say that what I did next was the result of a wise and well-thought-out plan, but it wasn't. It was simply one of those offhand but fortuitous questions that seems brilliant in retrospect. Knowing that, from a rational point of view, our company wasn't worth spending $150,000 to defend, I asked myself, 'What would Centerpointe look like if it was worth spending $150,000 in legal fees to defend?'

"In asking this question, I began to dream. 'Well,' I thought, 'if Centerpointe was worth spending $150,000 to defend, we would be advertising in national magazines. We would have a large headquarters filled with lots of activity and a lot of employees helping users of our programs to get the benefits we promise. I would be a published author and a sought-after speaker at conferences and seminars. We would have many thousands of customers all over the world, with millions of dollars in sales each year, and I would be a well-known expert in personal and spiritual growth. We would be one of the largest and most successful personal growth companies in the world.'

"As these improbable dreams occurred to me, I wrote them down and formulated a goal statement containing them. I found someone to help me create a magazine ad and placed it in a well-known magazine. To my surprise, it actually made money, so I placed the ad in another magazine, then another. Soon I was advertising in many national magazines.

"When orders started increasing, I bought out my business partner—who wanted out anyway—for one dollar and my promise to pay all the lawsuit costs, whatever they turned out to be. This gave me full control over the direction of the company.

"One by one, I worked on each piece of my dream, doggedly putting one foot in front of the other, week by week, month by month, and year by year, until everything I had envisioned had been accomplished. As I checked each item off the list, I added new and bigger dreams—and eventually checked those off, too. Fifteen years later, Centerpointe has the beautiful headquarters building I envisioned, a large number of employees, and over 160,000 people in 172 countries who have benefited from our programs. During those fifteen years, I published two books and wrote over 140 articles. I'm often invited to speak at conferences and seminars, just as I envisioned. I was even invited to speak at the United Nations on the subject of values.

"What's more, many educational institutions and researchers have studied or plan to study how our audio technology can have a positive effect on anxiety, depression, substance abuse, post-traumatic stress disorder, longevity, and a number of other conditions.

"The whole thing is truly amazing. The 'disaster' turned out to be a giant blessing in disguise. Without it, Centerpointe would probably have limped along for another year or so and then quietly gone to small business heaven. All of this happened because I looked for the potential benefits in what seemed at the time to be a major disaster, then took action to make those potential benefits a reality. In the process, I learned a huge lesson. When something 'bad' happens, if you focus on what you want, keep your mind off what you don't want or are worried about, and take action, then miraculous things can happen. Oh, yes. The lawsuit was settled with no money changing hands, and my legal fees cost me $7,000. My only concession in the settlement was for me to send a letter to my first forty-three customers telling them that our technology was not the same as our competitor's, a distinction I was happy to make!"[4]

Resiliency in Single Mothers

Single mothers must be highly resilient. Sometimes a new career emerges out of a struggle to be the sole wage earner and raise children alone. My father died when I was twelve and my sister was eight. My mother was hit hard by his death, even though he'd been sick for many months. We had no income and almost no savings. Despite her grief, she knew she had to find some way to support us. She'd married soon after graduating from high school and had always been a stay-at-home mom, so she had no marketable job skills. The best job she could find was working as a ward clerk at a nearby hospital. She knew she had to find a higher paying job, so she started taking secretarial classes at night school to qualify for a better job. Late at night, my sister and I could hear her practicing her typing lessons after we'd gone to bed.

Mom graduated and took a job at the hospital transcribing medical records. After ten years in medical records, she left the hospital to become office manager for three surgeons. Having grown up with two younger brothers that she had to help raise after her mother died, she was very good at managing men. She was so skillful with patients, doctors, and office staff, and at scheduling of surgeries, billings, collections, and record keeping, she became known as one of the best medical office managers in the area. The doctors needed her so much they included her in their retirement plan. In her later years, she felt especially proud about building up a retirement account that let her fully enjoy her retirement without ever being dependent on others.

• • • • • • • • • • • • • •

At age thirty-one, Suzy Kellett gave birth to quadruplets. When she brought the four babies home from the hospital, her husband couldn't handle all the crying, diaper changing, and feedings—not four babies all at once. He walked out, leaving Suzy in their Idaho home to care for the four infants by herself with no help and no income to pay the rent and other bills.

Suzy cried and cried. She was alone, penniless, and abandoned. But she wasn't helpless. She telephoned her parents in Illinois and told them what happened. They volunteered to take her and her babies into their home. Suzy packed up their few belongings and flew to Chicago—with nearby passengers on the flight helping to hold the infants.

Most people would have understood if this mother had drifted into self-pity, complaining how unfair life had been to her. She would be fully justified feeling bitter about her husband and blaming him for her plight.

During the first days back home, her parents took care of the babies when she withdrew into her room. She says, "Every so often my father would open my door and ask 'Scotch?' or 'Whiskey?' I'd start to chuckle and could feel his attitude helping me see that everything would be OK.

"I never allowed myself to wonder how my life would have been if I'd had only one baby. I knew that wouldn't be productive. I had the 'fabulous four.' I had to accept what was real.

"It helped that I came from a big family with lots of children. I was used to chaos. I never looked on that as a negative. I took a positive approach. I got everything organized with feedings, naps, laundry, and so forth so I wasn't dealing with random events all the time."

When Suzy searched for advice from other mothers with twins, triplets, or quadruplets, she couldn't find any. She paired up with a mother of triplets and together they started a national organization for parents with multiple births.

Her contacts with the media and efforts to spread information about their organization led to Suzy being offered a job with a television company. This experience eventually led to becoming director of a state office that coordinates motion picture productions. Today, Suzy's four children are all college graduates with successful careers of their own. Looking back on the entire experience, she says, "There were tough times, but I'd do it again because the good far outweighed the bad. And my humor really helped!"[5]

● ● ● ● ● ● ● ● ● ● ● ● ● ●

Resilient survivors handle their feelings well when hit with unexpected difficulties no matter how unfair. When hurt and distressed, they expect to eventually recover and find a way to have things turn out well. They bounce back after the bottom drops out of their lives, and often end up stronger and better than before.

Life Isn't Fair and That Can Be Good for You

Early in 1990, Tom Kelley was enjoying his position as vice president of human resources with Benjamin Franklin Savings and Loan. He had eighteen years of service with the S&L, owned stock in the corporation, and felt proud about how well his department had managed assimilating the employees from another savings-and-loan after it had been acquired.

The acquisition had been forced on the Benjamin Franklin by the US Treasury Department. The other S&L was in trouble and close to being shut down. Benjamin Franklin had a solid reputation and an excellent balance sheet from decades of conservative management. When the Benjamin Franklin directors said they didn't have the capitalization to acquire the other S&L, Treasury officials said the Benjamin Franklin could capitalize its name and count "good will" as an asset. With reluctance, the directors agreed. Tom's department worked hard to orient the acquired employees to the culture, values, and philosophy that had built the business.

Tom remembers Feb. 21, 1990, very well. When he arrived at work, he was told to come to a meeting with other senior managers in the boardroom. After they assembled, the president walked in, followed by seven somber-looking men in dark, pin-striped suits. The president announced that the Benjamin Franklin had been placed into receivership by the Resolution Trust Corporation (RTC). He said that new administrators at the Treasury had ruled that their "good will" could not be valued as an asset and that the Benjamin Franklin was undercapitalized.

"We were stunned," Tom says. "Treasury had reversed themselves. The managing agent of the RTC immediately replaced the president and our four top executives with RTC people who were brought in to try to manage a $5.5 billion-dollar organization. The place was in chaos. Employees didn't know who would stay or go. Our switchboard was flooded with calls from depositors. The branches had crowds of concerned people at their doors. What could our employees tell our customers? We didn't know ourselves if the Benjamin

Franklin would be shut down, broken up, sold, or what. The value of Benjamin Franklin stock plummeted to pennies.

"That first evening I asked myself, 'What information will my new boss need?' Overnight I put together a plan that included a complete list of all the people in every department and branch. I listed their years with the company and their responsibilities.

"It was hard to stay focused. I felt angry about what happened, fearful about the future, and distressed about what was happening to our employees. We had folks who had held their jobs for twenty years. They had no job-search skills. They needed major help. I talked with my new manager and persuaded him to approve hiring an excellent outplacement firm.

"I also could see that my position would be eliminated in the near future. I felt traumatized, uncertain about my future, insecure. How could I pay the mortgage? Provide for my family? Where could I work?

"I was told I had to leave the Benjamin Franklin in May of 1990. I have a lot of contacts. I found a position as director of human resources (HR) for a large insurance company, but it wasn't a good match. A year later, I told them that I was leaving. The executives were professional friends. They provided me with excellent transition support. I took extensive career-placement testing and interviews. I was surprised to learn that I had stronger aptitudes in marketing and sales than in HR. Career counseling led me to look for a position that combined sales and marketing with HR services.

"I set a goal of finding my ideal job in sixty days. I scheduled five interview appointments a day every day. I made finding my ideal job a full-time job, and I succeeded! I found a small consulting firm that provided human resources services for companies that need HR work but are too small to afford a full-time HR person. The company needed someone with a strong HR background who could market their services to this huge, untapped market. It was perfect for me.

"I started with them in December 1991. I feel such a passion for our products and services I lie awake at night excited about my work. At the time I started, they had eleven clients.

We now have over 1,000, and I'm on the executive team of a leading Northwest HR management consulting organization. I feel much better knowing I have more control over my future than I did working for large corporations.

"I'm glad I went through it. I was always self-confident, but I feel more self-confident now. I had to test my ability to hold up in crisis, persevere, set goals, and reach them. Now I know I can handle extreme difficulties. Before, I only hoped I could.

"The blessing from the Benjamin Franklin takeover is that I now have the ideal job for me. I now combine HR skills with my marketing talents and receive greater job satisfaction and more financial benefits!

"I believe things happen for a reason. No matter how chaotic and traumatic it may seem at the time, if you stay with it, with patience and persistence, there is a better opportunity around the corner. You must look for it."[6]

Eight Principles Affecting Your Resiliency

A consistent finding of the resiliency research is that attitudes and beliefs like those expressed by Tom Kelley play a key role in how resilient you may be. One the most powerful findings of the resiliency research is that internally directed, self-motivated people thrive in conditions of constant change. How much do the following principles reflect your beliefs?

1. When hit by life disrupting change, *you will never be the same again.* You will emerge either stronger or weaker, either better or bitter. You have within you the ability to determine which way it will be for you.

2. As you struggle with adversity or disruptive change, your mind and your habits will create barriers or bridges to a better future.

3. Blaming others for how bad things are for you keeps you in a non-resilient victim state in which you do not take resiliency actions.

4. Life isn't fair, and that can be very good for you. Resiliency comes from feeling personally responsible for

finding a way to overcome the adversity. Your struggle to bounce back and recover from setbacks can lead to developing strengths and abilities you didn't know you were capable of.

5. Your unique resiliency strengths develop from self-motivated, self-managed learning in the school of life.

6. Self-knowledge enhances your resiliency because your way of being resilient must be your own self-created, unique version. Self-knowledge comes from self-observation, experimenting, and being receptive to feedback of all kinds.

7. The observing place within you is where you develop conscious choices about how you will interact with the world you live in. Experiencing choices leads to feelings of freedom, independence, and being in control of your life.

8. As you become more and more resilient, you effectively handle disruptive change, adversities, and major setbacks faster and easier.[7]

The guidelines for developing resiling skills provided in this book show how to become as resilient as you wish. Your energy for being resilient comes from living in ways that optimize your health and well-being. The next chapter, about Level One resiliency, covers how to cope effectively with many pressures and live a healthy lifestyle. It shows how to retain control of your life during difficult times of change, and free yourself from cultural myths about "stress."

Resiliency Development Activities

1. Interview several people who have been through extremely difficult experiences and express positive feelings about what they went through. Ask them why they don't feel like victims. Find out what they did to turn things around and how they are able to appreciate what they went through.

2. Do you allow your environment to control you, or do you feel that your responses are under your control and that you can influence your environment? What are examples of both ways of reacting that you've experienced?

3. Notice how Bill Harris used questions to pull himself through his business crisis as did Cynthia Dailey-Hewkin (Chapter 1). Marilee Adams, author of *Change Your Questions, Change Your Life,* discovered early in her professional life the value of what she calls "question thinking." She found first for herself, and then with her clients, that asking the right questions can transform a person's life from feeling like a victim to creating a path for bouncing back.[9] When you are faced with a crisis or challenge, start listing resiliency questions.

4. Review the list of the eight principles affecting how resilient you may become. Reflect on how much each one is relevant to you. How much or how little do you believe they are true? Are there other principles you see as affecting how resilient a person can be? Discuss these principles with several people who identify with resiliency as being important to them.

Chapter Four

Optimize Your Health:
A Practical Action Plan

Dr. Hans Selye, the physician who conducted the pioneering research about "biological stress," apologized after he retired for making a serious mistake. In his autobiography, he confessed that "stress" was the wrong term. He said he should have called his research findings the "strain syndrome."[1]

The widespread belief about jobs having harmful stress is an artificial "consensus reality." Articles, books, and workshops about stress, while well-intentioned, sustain an illusion that something called "stress" is constantly assaulting and harming us.[2]

The difference in meaning between stress and strain is an example of how our minds can put up barriers or build bridges to resiliency. What most people call *stress* is really an internal, physical feeling of anxiety or *strain* that they don't like. This is not just semantics. Stress is the external pressure, strain is the internal effect.

One consequence of false beliefs about stress is that many employees have been misled into blaming their working conditions for their feelings of distress and do not try to develop resiliency strengths. Your ability to hold up under pressure is strengthened when you understand that unpleasant strains experienced at work or in your private life are your personal, subjective reactions. In a high-pressure job, you can choose to cope well with the strains and work with strength, or you can allow yourself to react like a weak, helpless victim.

The ability of our minds to observe what is happening and then create choices for effective responding is what makes humans different from animals and makes modern humans different from our ancestors. Our minds and attitudes can convert threats into challenges that energize us in healthy ways.

We Differ in How Much Strain We Can Handle

Human beings vary widely in how much weight they can lift. American weightlifter Shane Hammon has lifted over 1,000 pounds, but an elderly person might not be able to lift 10. Similarly, people vary widely in how much strain they can handle. A police lieutenant working the night shift in a suburb of Los Angeles, told me his job is boring. "It's been fourteen years of the same old thing," he said. "Every night it's convenience store holdups, auto accidents, break-ins, suicide threats, bar fights, drug sales, gang shootings, family disputes....It's the same boring thing every night. I'm thinking of taking early retirement to do my photography hobby full-time. I have my own darkroom at home. That would excite me."

Selye studied the physiology of "being sick." He described a living creature's physiological responses to sustained, biologically overtaxing demands as a three-stage General Adaptation Syndrome:[3]

+ the Alarm Reaction
+ the Stage of Resistance
+ the Stage of Exhaustion

The Alarm Reaction is our emergency alert system. It is the fight or flight response that helped our ancestors survive in hostile environments where predators or enemies might approach unnoticed and suddenly attack.

When you feel anger or fright, hormones from the adrenal glands instantly prepare your body for emergency action. Your blood sugar becomes elevated, and your heart rate speeds up to pump blood to your muscles for instant fighting or a short burst of running. Your red blood cells become "sticky" to increase clotting if you are wounded. The pupils in your eyes widen, you breathe harder and faster, and you perspire. At the same time, the activities of the parasympathetic nervous system, the "repair and heal" system, are suppressed. Immune-system functions decrease and digestion slows down.

When people feel constantly threatened, angry, or anxious, their sympathetic nervous system keeps them in an agitated condition of emergency arousal. If sympathetic nervous system arousal continues unabated for weeks and months, diseases of adaptation develop—high blood pressure, heart attacks, strokes, bleeding ulcers, and cancer—leading to premature death, if not reversed.

Events may trigger an emergency response and always should. We need to have a physiological emergency response for getting us out of a burning building or carrying a child through floodwaters. But in modern life, the fight or flight biological heritage that saved our ancestors is shortening lives. Researchers in Finland found that 22,430 public-sector employees who kept their jobs after major layoffs and downsizing were sick more often and that their death rate from cardiovascular disease doubled.[4]

The challenge for us in a rapidly changing, fast-paced world is to learn how to intersperse periods of sympathetic nervous system arousal with periods of parasympathetic, repairing and healing activities. To remain healthy, your body needs times when your heart rate slows down, digestive processes increase, and the complex activities of your immune system increase. Parasympathetic activity is a physiological process that can be influenced indirectly, but not directly. It functions best when you leave it alone and allow it to work without your conscious efforts.

Your Optimal Health Plan

The Optimal Health Plan that follows shows how to retain psychological control and take advantage of new information about mind-body connections that increase health and well-being.[5] When you use this Optimal Health Plan, you will experience many benefits. You will manage your emotional reactions in emotionally competent ways, gain control over events in your life that affect you, and be able to create a positive, supportive, healthy environment for yourself.

Part One: Write Two Lists:
"What is Difficult for Me?"

Make a list of six or seven things that you feel irritated, upset, or distressed about. Ask and answer questions such as

+ What pressures am I feeling?
+ How is my work and my life different than it was a year ago?
+ What is difficult for me now and what difficulties am I expecting?
+ What feels distressing to me?

Take your time and be thorough. Write descriptive phrases. During a resiliency seminar, a group of federal civil-service employees working for the US Navy listed these pressures:

+ Our work group has been downsized by 30%, but we are still expected to do the same amount of work as before.

+ We've heard that the top brass might downsize us again.

+ Our operating budget has been cut twice.

+ The Department of Defense replaced our old computer system and software program with new computers and new software that work slower than the old system. It's exhausting trying to get more work done with a software program that has increased the time it takes to do our work.

+ Because we have fewer employees and problems with the new computer system, delays have increased angry phone calls and urgent demands from high-ranking officers. Working on their emergencies takes time away from getting our assigned work done.

+ We must also take time away from our assigned work, to keep hourly, detailed, written records of our job activities, because the Department of Defense is considering "outsourcing" our entire unit to an outside contractor.

+ We feel trapped. In the past, pay increases did not keep up with cost-of-living increases, and now we hear that cost-of-living pay increases will be eliminated and changed over to a merit pay system. We're losing ground compared to pay levels in private industry. Many of us are too old to walk away from our retirement packages to start a new career elsewhere, and we're too young to qualify for early retirement.

+ We're worried about the effects of all this stress on our health.

Notice that these workers listed as a stressor worrying about the effects of many job stresses. During the workshop, they felt more emotionally free and empowered when they learned about the false consensus reality about "job stress." Our discussion about who is responsible for how a person reacts to life events led most of the group to stop blaming their commanders and the Department of Defense for their reactions to all the pressures, and start accepting responsibility for their reactions.[6]

"I feel…"

The next step is to talk or write about how you feel about the items you listed. During difficult times, an important resiliency step is being able to express your feelings in healthy ways.

You can't make feelings go away, but you can move through them. As shown in the diagram in chapter 1, resilient people express what they feel upset about as a step toward regaining a positive frame of mind needed for bouncing back. If you were raised to be a "good child," to always be happy and never complain, writing such a list may be hard to do. If you work in a "macho" occupation such as construction, law enforcement, or fire fighting, there may be a group norm that regards talking or writing about feelings as a sign of weakness. Expressing your feelings, however, is as important as the maintenance work you know you must do on equipment your life depends on.

A few years ago, a group of older professional workers lost their jobs because of corporate downsizing and had not been successful in becoming re-employed after a year of searching. Psychologist James Pennebaker and his associates had them write about their emotions for twenty minutes each day for two weeks. Eight months after the writing sessions, two thirds of the participants had full-time or satisfactory part-time employment. During that same time period, less than one third of a comparable, non-writing group found employment.

Pennebaker reports that all the people in the group who wrote about their feelings said they wished they had written about their feelings sooner. They realized they had not done well in job interviews during the previous year because they had not handled their feelings well. Research with many other groups has documented improved coping abilities when people under pressure write about their feelings regularly. The better you become at being able to recognize, verbalize, and manage your feelings, the less you will be vulnerable to losing emotional control or developing cardiovascular illnesses.[7]

Now List Your Positive Experiences

After listing and writing about negative, distressing challenges, switch over and make a second list of positive experiences you enjoy. List activities that revitalize and invigorate you. Ask yourself these questions:

- ✦ What do I have fun doing? What do I get enthusiastic about?
- ✦ What would I like to do that I keep putting off?
- ✦ Who do I enjoy sharing good experiences with?
- ✦ When do I sleep best at night?
- ✦ What positive aspects of my life am I ignoring?

Part Two: Take Action

Decide to Cope Well with Challenges

After you've made your lists about what drains you and what revitalizes you, you are at a choice point. Are you going to take action or not take action to reduce your distressing, energy-draining experiences and increase pleasant, revitalizing experiences? Here's why this question is important:

In the 1960s, research psychologists began to investigate people who coped well with life's difficulties and were more stress resistant than others. Richard Lazarus discovered that people who cope well focus outward to problem solve their difficulties. Julian Rotter (covered in chapter 3) found that self-motivated people who feel capable of taking effective action when threatened hold up much better than people who have a fatalistic attitude and believe their lives are controlled by forces out of their control.

In the 1970s, some psychologists began to study the connection between internal, locus of control attitudes and fewer stress-related health problems. In 1975, University of Chicago Professor Salvatore Maddi began a twelve-year study of 450 male and female managers and executives at Illinois Bell Telephone, a subsidiary of the American Telephone and Telegraph company (AT&T). During the study, the US Department of Justice prosecuted an antitrust lawsuit that led to breaking up the AT&T corporation into seven "baby Bells."

These were trying times for Bell system managers and executives. Shock waves rippled through the Bell system. Thousands of stockholders panicked. Retirees, widows, and investors with large holdings in trusts and mutual funds flooded Bell offices with phone calls and letters. Illinois Bell was downsized from 26,000 to 14,000 employees.[8]

The Maddi research team found that two thirds of the executives and managers in the study showed signs of the General Adaptation Syndrome. They had heart attacks, strokes, gastrointestinal ulcers, and many illnesses related to immune system depletion, such as arthritis and cancer. This group also had migraine headaches, anxiety attacks, depression, alcoholism, substance abuse, angry tantrums, and a few suicides. Many reported feeling confused, fearful, worried, distrustful of management, overwhelmed, powerless, low energy, and pessimistic. In the workplace. they had more absenteeism, received poor performance reviews, and some demotions.

The other one third in the study, however, did not show debilitating effects—just the opposite. They remained healthy and happy, felt enlivened, developed better relationships at home and at work, had excellent performance reviews, and received promotions. This group, called the "hardy" ones, thrived in the chaos that was distressing and ruinous for others. They were more than stress resistant; they seemed to be immune to the same workplace conditions experienced as stressful, destructive, and harmful by their co-workers.

The Illinois Bell researchers found that the hardy executives and managers had three qualities:

+ They made an emotional *commitment* to do their best to successfully handle the ongoing events, and to help others as well.

+ They believed they could influence the outcomes and actively worked to reach specific goals. This gave them a feeling of being in *control* of their job assignments and their part of the action.

+ They felt energized and *challenged* to solve the problems and cope effectively with every difficulty.[9]

The hardiness research by Maddi and his associates confirmed Rotter's original research and what many other psychologists have found: people who feel in control hold up much better and remain healthier in high-pressure, disruptive change. Your Optimal Health Plan emphasizes ways to gain control of how you respond to pressures, extreme change, and challenges.

Decrease Negative Experiences

Look at your list of negative experiences. Pick one item and create an action plan to feel less vulnerable and more in control. Decide to find a way to decrease the negative effect it has on you. Ask questions such as

- What if I ignored this? What if I avoided contact?
- Could I do something about this? What could I do to change how it bothers me?
- Can I make it go away? Can I get it out of my life?

If you feel micromanaged by your boss, learn how to deal effectively with managers who micromanage in ways that impair worker effectiveness.[10]

If negative talk in the lunch room at work is getting you down, you could go for a walk instead of listening to all the complaining. If you feel distressed seeing pictures of wounded and dead people on evening television news broadcasts, turn off the TV set and listen to music.

Ask yourself: If I can't avoid it, change it, or make it go away, what if I changed my response to it? What if I decided to stop letting it bother me?

You feel strained only by what you emotionally and physically attempt to deal with. Disengaging yourself from some things around you conserves your resiliency energy for more important challenges.

To gain control over your automatic reactions and develop choices for action, become an observer. If you pause to observe how you typically react, you can create choices for responding in a different way.

How do you do this? Watch with curiosity the ways that you react to others. What is typical for you? Become a witness, as though you are recording a dramatic play on a videotape. Replay the tape and observe your role. Then, as the scriptwriter, come up with several possibilities for responding differently.

Being able to pause and observe before you take action is an essential part of this strategy. Develop several choices about how to respond, then choose one that you feel would let you gain control, feel less vulnerable, and lead to an outcome that you would feel good about.

Once you feel that you have made good progress with one item on your list, select another. Don't try to do them all at once. If you do, it will be like making a long list of New Year's resolutions and then noticing in March that you have not accomplished any of them.

Revise Your Theme Song

A clue that you have set up the dramas in your life as being beyond your control is when you believe that your life will improve when other people change how they talk, think, and act. I have heard this assertion stated so many times, I call it "The Theme Song of the Human Race." The chorus of the song is "If only other people would change, things would be much better for me."

This is a true statement, of course. I agree that if only certain people would change the way they think, talk, and act, you could feel less distress and more happiness. No question about that.

But what are the probabilities that others are going to voluntarily change their ways of talking and acting so that your life will be better?

The answers I get in my workshops are "Zero." "None." "Zip."

The point here is that the Theme Song is correct, but it also empowers difficult people to control you. If you blame others for causing your feelings of distress and conclude that improvement will come only when they change, you are locking yourself into a helpless victim pattern.

So what can be done? I start by owning the problem I'm experiencing. If you feel off-balance, vulnerable, or frustrated when others act or talk in ways that you can't handle well, that's OK. This situation can open a path to learning new and better ways of responding.

The key to making your life better is to stop blaming others for triggering reactions in you that you don't like. The problem is not what others do; it is your reaction to what they do. Focus instead on learning better ways to respond. When you learn effective responses, your emotional strain is reduced.

Write a new theme song for yourself. The chorus may be something like "Everyone gets to do what they do, and I get to learn how to not let them bother me." Each new verse will be for a specific challenge on your list.

If you feel upset by what others do or say, try seeing the situation as a test in the school of life. Look at it as an opportunity to learn about your blind spots. Appreciate chances to learn better ways of handling people who knock you off-balance emotionally.

Ask for Support

Can you ask for help when you need it? If you have always been the strong one in your family, it is all right to ask the family for help, emotional support, and encouragement. They will probably love you all the more. They may be glad to see you stop trying to be the strong one always in control.

Research into health and illness is leading to what is called a "biopsychosocial" model of health. Everything you think and feel has an effect on your physical health; the quality of your interactions with others has an effect on your physical health. As studied by psychologist Sheldon Cohen, social support can come to you in three ways:

1. Help with daily tasks, providing food and supplies, or financial assistance.
2. Advice, guidance, and problem solving.
3. Listening, caring, empathy, and reassurance.[11]

You recover better when you tell your family, a friend, or a support group what you are feeling. If you'd like them just to listen and not problem solve while you talk, let them know. If you want some suggestions and coaching on what to do, let them know that. A friend will listen, sympathize, and won't tell you not to feel what you are feeling. If you cry—and that may be helpful—he or she will wait until you are done.

If you feel overwhelmed and lack energy for handling the pressures, consider seeking professional help. Take this suggestion seriously. Anyone who tries to act as though he or she never feels upset or distressed is more fragile than people who admit they need counseling.

Increase Positive Experiences

Decreasing negative experiences is only half of your action plan. Increasing your positive experiences is actually more important than decreasing your negative ones. Pleasant, positive experiences revitalize you, boost your immunity to emotional toxicity, and give you more strength to sustain yourself in adverse circumstances. Whatever you choose to do, it's important that the activity completely absorbs you. Lose yourself in what you are doing and forget about all else.

Divide your list of activities for enhancing your health and well-being into active and passive. Active health enhancement includes *physical activities* such as jogging, bike riding, hiking, playing recreational sports, gardening, enjoying a hobby, playing a musical instrument, doing tai chi, qigong, yoga, or aerobic workouts.

Dozens of people who held up well under extreme pressure, in a variety of circumstances, were interviewed by psychiatrist William Glasser to find out how they avoided burnout. He found that most of them had a "positive addiction." They had a favorite activity such as bike riding or jogging that they felt compelled to do.[12]

Pleasant, revitalizing *emotional activities* may include spending time with a close friend, taking children to places they enjoy, cooking a meal for someone you like, enjoying a family celebration, watching videotapes that make you laugh, or doing something special with a loved one. Cohen's research shows that people with a happy family life and lots of friends remain healthier than people with poor relationships. Anything you do playfully is revitalizing. Laughing is a powerful healer.

The healing and repairing processes in your body do their best work when you do nothing. *Passive activities* include sitting and listening to music with your eyes closed, meditating, getting a massage, relaxing in a hot tub or sauna, taking a nap, resting, or sitting outside doing nothing—all of this while keeping your mind silent and fully enjoying the sensations of the moment.

Use a Plan That Fits Your Nature

To increase your immune system activity, it helps to know your inborn predispositions. For example, do you tend to be introverted or extroverted? Socially extroverted people recover from setbacks best by talking with others. Physically extroverted people need intense physical stimulation and lots of action. Introverted people need time alone, away from others. Trying to use a recovery style incompatible with your inborn predisposition may strain you further.

Every individual's way of sustaining their health and energy must fit them. A woman I know sold her business, ended a relationship with a man, sold her home, moved to another state, and started a new career at lower pay. She stayed healthy because she knew she was at risk and took very good care of herself. She went for walks, took naps, got massages, spent time with good friends, wrote about her feelings in a personal journal, ate healthy foods, laughed a lot, got plenty of sleep, and held off starting a new career for a few months.

There are no rules on how to do it right. What one person says worked for him or her may not fit with what you need to do. You will have to experiment to discover what is best for you.

To create your customized plan

+ Look at your list of what revitalizes you.
+ Think of ways to repeat, increase, or have new positive experiences.
+ Develop a plan of action for increasing positive, revitalizing experiences.
+ Do what revitalizes and nourishes you. Do what renews you and lets you sleep better.

Factors Influencing Health and Well-Being

Some people live a lifestyle that almost seems designed to make them become ill or lead to shortening their lives.[13] The following list summarizes research findings about what people do who are *less* likely to develop illnesses. People who remain healthy under pressure

+ experience little distress in routine activities;
+ feel in control of their lives and capable of taking effective action about what upsets them;
+ draw action choices from a wide range of inner and external resources;

- enjoy good relationships with family and friends;
- know how they feel and can express feelings;
- accept responsibility for their responses to what others do and say;
- manage self-change well;
- develop healthy lifestyle habits;
- convert negative experiences into beneficial learning;
- actively pursue positive, enjoyable experiences.[14]

Do your actions match this list? If so, congratulate yourself. If not, this list provides guidelines on what you need to work on.

A related factor to examine is your expectation about how long you think you will live. How long do people in your family expect to live? Do you have any old-timers? Many families do not.

Experts on longevity say that in optimal conditions, we humans can live for 110 to 120 years in good health. As medical care improves and people become smarter about how to sustain optimal health, the average length of life is increasing. Statistical predictions project that by the year 2030, there will be over one million people in the United States 100 years of age or over. Many will *not* be in nursing homes or assisted living facilities. Can you imagine yourself being one of them?[15]

Enjoy Strain Like a Good Workout

Notice that the Optimal Health Plan does not say to avoid pressure or strain. We know from Dr. Selye's research, that we need a moderate amount of strain to remain healthy. Selye called it "eustress" meaning "good stress." Without periods of strain we lose strength and deteriorate. People confined to bed for long periods lose muscle tone. Astronauts lose bone mass and muscle strength during weeks aboard the International Space Station outside the strain of earth's gravity.

An optimal plan has you alternating the strains of intense work with periods of detachment, rest, and relaxation. Alternating strain with relaxation sustains your health and increases strength.[16]

To achieve deep relaxation, Dr. Herbert Benson suggests learning to stay relaxed while doing simple repetitive tasks or going for strolls. He also recommends taking long, slow, deep breaths to relax. With practice, you can use one deep breath to calm yourself quickly any time, any place.[17]

If driving to work and back puts you into rush hour traffic, relax and flow with the stops and surges. Expect a few drivers to try to gain a few seconds by squeezing in ahead of you when there is no space. Let them do that while you listen to relaxing music or audio books.

A young woman working at a copy center I've often been to looked more frazzled than usual one day. I asked her how things were going. She complained about how hectic her job was with no letup from all the impatient customers. I said "Here, I'll write you a prescription."

I wrote "BREATHE" on one of her sticky notes and handed it to her. I said, "Place this on the side of the copy machine where you can see it while you are waiting for a job to finish. Stand quietly when you notice it. Mentally disengage from the action at the counter for a few moments. Take several slow, deep breaths. Count to five each time you inhale and exhale."

The next time I came in she grinned and said "Your breathing prescription is super! I'm not worn out at the end of the day, the way I used to be."

Few people breathe well. If you look at any group of people, most of their breathing is shallow—even people who drink from bottles of water because they know that keeping our cells hydrated slows aging and sustains energy. Humans can survive for up to five days without water, but less than five minutes without oxygen. Oxygenating your blood and cells is far more important than hydrating them. Breathe.

Summary

The science of resiliency includes these understandings:

+ You can increase your resiliency when you free your mind from the illusion of "stress."

+ People differ in their perceptions, attitudes, and explanations about their circumstances. The least resilient people experience normal working conditions as hostile and harmful. The most resilient people experience the same working conditions as safe and enjoyable.

+ People differ in how much they feel able to take action to create an optimal environment for themselves. Some people who feel distressed by their circumstances do not believe that personal effort could make anything better. Others feel personally responsible for how well their lives go and that they can keep learning new ways to handle things better. They know that they can exercise some control over events and how they respond to events.

+ As biological creatures, we have automatic reflexes to perceived threats that trigger sympathetic nervous system responses. By knowing this and seeing why it is useful to understand your inborn survival biology, you can observe what triggers your emergency alarm reactions. You can ask yourself why you feel threatened and decide to accept responsibility for your reactions. The more you know about mind-body interactions, the more you can consciously choose to act in ways that sustain your health and energy.[18]

+ People differ in how much emotional and physiological strain is optimal. Some thrive in high levels of pressure and strain that would cause heart attacks, ulcers, and illnesses in others. Some people function best in low-pressure, tranquil circumstances that would be distressingly unstimulating and boring for others.

+ Optimal health isn't something you have to chase or work

hard to develop. Optimal health is what you enjoy when you live in ways that don't harm your body and allow your body time to repair and heal. Long periods of emergency alert, autonomic nervous system arousal can lead to serious health problems if not interspersed with time for the parasympathetic nervous system to repair and heal. People differ in which activities are most useful for them.

✦ Your Optimal Health Plan for decreasing distressing experiences and increasing revitalizing ones will prevent feelings of helplessness and hopelessness. As you become better and better at handling your emotional reactions in emotionally competent ways, you strengthen your emotional immunity to events that distress others and increase your resiliency.

✦ As you become better at handling feelings such as anger, pessimism, and discouragement, you are less easily pulled off-balance by those feelings in others. If you don't handle your own feelings well, you can't handle being exposed to those feelings in others very well.

Keep in mind that time plays a part in this. Certain pressures can be changed today; others will take weeks and months. Some pleasant activities may take awhile to arrange.

The practical, Optimal Health Plan outlined in this chapter can bring you many benefits. It will reduce your unpleasant experiences and increase the kinds of positive experiences that can sustain your health and well-being a long, long time. And, as you will see in the next chapter, the enjoyment of many positive feelings also improves your problem-solving skills.

Resiliency Development Activities

1. If you'd like a job and a life with less strain, you can have it:

   ▷ Create a personal plan to optimize your emotional and physical health. Do things to support your health and well-being in ways that are simple, easy, and natural for you.

▷ Increase your feelings of control over how you respond to the external demands and activities that you choose to handle well.

▷ Decide to free your mind from the widespread consensus reality about stress. Stress is only a concept. It's an abstract idea. Focus instead, on exactly what your ears hear and your eyes see.

▷ Notice what triggers emotional reactions in you. Imagine yourself remaining relaxed, amused, or indifferent the next time.

▷ Mentally rehearse your new, preferred response and notice how you feel.

▷ Look forward to the next time a previous "stressor" occurs so that if it happens again, you can use your positive, resiliency response instead of feeling distressed or helpless.

▷ Notice times when you enjoy mental and physical strains.

▷ Pause after a period of strain to take several long, deep, relaxing breaths. Deep breathing should include exhaling fully. The strain/breathe/relax, strain/breathe/relax, strain/breathe/relax sequence will have many beneficial effects.

▷ At the end of each day, reflect on how good you feel about handling strains and challenges easily and naturally.

2. An additional benefit from handling pressure and change well is that you can help others cope well. You can do this by asking someone that you care about these two questions: "How are you feeling about what is happening?" and "What are you doing to take care of yourself?" When you ask these two questions and take time to listen, the people you care about will feel better and cope better. Do this the next chance you get and see what happens.

Chapter Five

Skillfully Problem Solve

My grandfather was a cheery old guy, despite all the hard times he'd lived through—the Depression in the 1930s, two World Wars, working at odd jobs from early morning until after dark because his small farm couldn't support his large family, the death of two wives, and more. He'd gained a lot of practical intelligence from his many life experiences. He would tell us stories about difficulties he'd trouble-shooted on jobs, on his farms, and with people.

Grandpa came to live with us when I was a boy. If some difficulty arose, he'd shake his head and say, "Yup, life is one darned thing after another." Then he'd say, "Let's see what we can do to remedy this."

The second level of resiliency to master is based on research showing that people who focus on solving the problems they encounter are much more resilient than people who disengage, feel helpless, or become highly emotional. When you are hit with a setback or unexpected difficulty, it is in your best interests to focus on dealing effectively with the challenge. People who become highly emotional in the middle of a crisis do not cope well with adversities.

Pioneering research conducted by psychologist Richard Lazarus established that effective coping includes both *emotion-focused* coping and *problem-focused* coping.[1] The connection between a problem-solving response and resiliency has been confirmed many times. Research conducted by Mary Steinhardt at a division of the Motorola corporation found that employees who use problem-focused coping in a constantly changing work environment are more resilient, have good relationships with others, and enjoy better health. Steinhardt's study also confirmed that the least resilient people do not cope well with their unhappy feelings, believe their jobs are full of stress, and have more illnesses.[2]

Let's look closer at the issue of expressing feelings. In the previous chapter on Level One resiliency, the ability to express feelings of distress was described as an important health-enhancing activity. If that is true, why are emotional reactions now described as counterproductive? According to psychologists Annette Stanton and Robert Franz, it is poor timing, amplification of feelings, and disengagement that can make emotional reactions maladaptive. When hit by a crisis, some people disengage from the challenges at hand by amplifying their emotional reactions. It isn't that reacting emotionally is wrong; they just do it at the worst possible time in the worst possible place. Some people react in dramatic, attention-getting ways at the slightest opportunity and often blame others for causing their feelings.[3]

The most resilient people, in contrast, control their emotional reactions in a crisis, engage the problems, then process their feelings afterward. C. R. Snyder reviewed hundreds of studies about human coping skills. He points out that problem-focused and emotion-focused coping can be mutually facilitating. When both are well done, they enhance each other.[4]

Problem-focused coping starts with examining a situation, developing an accurate understanding of exactly what the problem is, and clarifying what outcomes you want. You consider various ways to get from where you are to where you want to be, select the best choice, and take action. You observe the effects of the action to quickly learn what is working or not working. Then you modify your actions to get the best results.

Help Your Brain, Have Fun

Before we cover different ways to problem solve, it is important to see that there is another connection between Level One resiliency activities and problem solving. Research by psychologist Barbara Frederickson shows positive emotions broaden a person's cognitive skills. Positive emotions make you more aware of many things happening. You notice small details and can remember many tasks that have to be done. This means that feelings such as enjoyment, playfulness, contentment, job satisfactions, love, and affection, as well as laughing and warm moments with friends, all increase mental abilities essential to problem solving. Negative emotions, in contrast, decrease resiliency. Feelings such as anxiety, anger, fear, vulnerability, and helplessness narrow cognitive functions and limit action choices.

Frederickson describes her findings as the "broaden and build" theory of positive emotions. The "build" part comes from her finding that certain kinds of enjoyable activities increase resiliency strengths. Play, for instance, builds physical skills, self-mastery, understanding, and improves health. Enjoyable times with friends strengthens one's immune system and increases social resources that are available during difficult times.

Frederickson also found that the strengths gained during positive states are durable: they last a long time in the face of adversity and ongoing difficulties. Negative emotions, on the other hand, weaken a person's endurance.[5]

Notice that the desirable positive emotions come directly from your everyday experiences. It is important to distinguish these from temporary pleasant *sensations* such as eating ice cream, drinking alcohol, or doing drugs.

The point here is that you can increase your problem-solving capacities when you purposefully experience many positive emotions each day. Taking time to laugh, appreciate pleasant moments, and "smell the roses" daily affects your brain and nervous system in ways that enhance your problem-solving skills, and this in turn increases your resiliency.

You Can Use Three Kinds of Intelligence to Problem Solve

Robert Sternberg and his colleagues have conducted worldwide research to understand three kinds of intelligence that determine success in life. Sternberg, in his presidential address to the American Psychological Association in 2003, described three identifiably different kinds of intelligence used by people in almost every culture:

+ Analytical intelligence—logic, reason, and abstract thinking used to solve familiar problems

+ Creative intelligence—used to invent unusual solutions in new and unfamiliar circumstances

+ Practical intelligence—applied to solving situational, real-life problems. People who are "street smart" are individuals who have practical intelligence, although they may use logical and creative thinking as well.[6]

Analytical Problem Solving

Problem solving of any kind always involves asking questions. Here are steps for using analysis, logic, and reasoning to problem solve in circumstances you are familiar with:

First, develop an accurate understanding of the nature of the threat, challenge, or difficulty. You accomplish this by asking questions such as: What is the problem? What are the facts? How serious is it? How urgent is it? How much time do I have? What additional information do I need? Is this a problem I can do anything about? Must I be the one who takes action?

Second, ask yourself, What do I want? What is my goal? What kind of outcome would satisfy me? Does my goal take into account everyone who would be affected?

There's an old psychology story about an elderly retired man who was bothered by noisy boys playing outside the window of his small, first-floor apartment. Did he yell at them to go away? No. That wouldn't have been smart. He went outside and said he loved hearing boys play and that he would give them each a quarter to play under his window. The boys were delighted. He paid them a quarter every day for a week. The second week he came out after they had been playing and explained that because he was very poor, he could only afford a dime for each of them. The boys didn't like the reduction in their payment. Several left, but most of them stayed. At the beginning of the third week, the retired gentleman came out and explained that he was so poor he could afford only a penny for each of them each day. The boys left, saying they wouldn't play near his window for pennies. The elderly man's strategy for solving his problem reflected an accurate understanding of how his actions would affect the boys.

Third, outline two or more possible ways to overcome the problem to achieve a positive outcome. Then look at the risks and potential negative effects of each of your solutions. If you have time, it is very useful to discuss the possible solutions with a friend, colleague, or mentor.

Fourth, take action. It is normal to feel a bit anxious when you do or say something you have never done before. Keep in mind that if you knew exactly what to do about a difficulty, it wouldn't be a problem!

Fifth, look at the effects of the action you have taken. Ask questions aimed at getting accurate feedback. If you are working on a problem that will take a long time to resolve, then look for small indications that things are moving in the right direction. In organizations, it can take weeks or months to reach a satisfactory resolution of a problem.

Sixth, learn from the feedback you get. Reappraise your understanding of the problem and the situation.

Seventh, modify your efforts. When what you are doing isn't working, do something else!

Eighth, reevaluate the outcome. Is it satisfactory to you? Can you now leave the situation and move on to other things?

Ninth, ask yourself what you learned from this. Were there early clues that you ignored? What were the lessons here for you? How can you avoid having to deal with a similar problem again in the future?

● ● ● ● ● ● ● ● ● ● ● ● ● ● ●

The steps for rational problem solving are useful in situations that can be analyzed. In one of my workshops, an operations manager for a transit system (I'll call him Matt) told the class that he was under pressure to reduce his costs. Matt studied the budget expenditures and saw that the annual cost for paper towels in the operations budget was over $25,000. "Why is this cost so high?" he wondered. "Is there petty theft taking place?" He didn't think so.

Matt spent several weeks in the bus barns observing the drivers and the bus-cleaning crews. He noted everything done with the paper towels.

Bus drivers are responsible for keeping their busses clean during their shifts. When the drivers came on duty, Matt saw each one pick up a new package of paper towels from the supply room on the way to their assigned bus. During their shifts, the drivers would break open the package of towels and clean up messes left by passengers on the hand rails and seats. At the end of their shifts, the drivers would leave the partially used packages of towels on the bus.

The bus-cleaning crews were responsible for removing all trash. For them, this meant removing the partially used bundles of paper towels and throwing them out. When Matt looked in the dumpsters, he saw large stacks of unused paper towels thrown into the trash.

Here was the problem. One package of towels for each driver, every shift, every day, added up to a major expense.

The drivers needed the paper towels. He understood that, but he believed the system could be changed to reduce the huge amount of waste. He outlined several solutions and discussed them with his boss.

The solution they decided to implement was to purchase small dispensers, one-half the size of a bundle of towels, and have them installed on each bus. He then gave the cleaning crews responsibility for keeping the dispensers filled. Now, instead of discarding the unused towels, they would keep the ones left over.

Matt says the cost of paper towels dropped immediately. His solution saved the transit system over $6000 a year in the cost of towels. And after several years, he got the budget director to transfer the cost of the towels from the operations budget to the supplies budget.

Matt followed all the steps for rational problem solving. He identified the problem, was clear about the desired goal, collected information, considered several solutions, took action, evaluated the results, and was satisfied with the outcome.

* * * * * * * * * * * * * * *

Analytical problem solving can be developed as a habitual way of responding to daily challenges. Sometimes it takes only several minutes.

One hot July afternoon, I was teaching a resiliency workshop for a national corporation at their training center near Chicago. The outside temperature was over 90 degrees Fahrenheit. My classroom was on the sunny side of the building and was very hot because the air conditioning unit in our room was not working. The participants and I had turned the thermostat down to 70 degrees, but the air conditioning unit, located under the window, did not respond.

One participant dramatically fanned himself with a piece of paper, with a look on his face indicating that he was irritated by his discomfort. You've probably seen people who do this. They become irritated by small discomforts and draw attention to themselves in ways that indicate they believe that someone is not paying attention to their needs.

Meanwhile, a participant named Brian went over to the air conditioner. He lifted up a small panel on the top and looked down into the dim interior. It was an older unit, without clear markings. He saw a dusty black knob located near the bottom of the unit, about two feet down. He reached down and turned it. As soon as he did this, the air conditioner kicked on. Our room soon cooled down, and we held the class in comfort.

At the first break, we went to other classrooms on our floor to show other instructors how to cool down their sweltering rooms. None of them had problem solved the air conditioning difficulty the way that Brian had done in my classroom. Brian had looked at the thermostat on the wall and at the air conditioner under the window and assumed that it was constructed so that most people could figure out how to make it work. He assumed that he could figure out what to do and acted in a way that solved the problem.

It was a great opportunity for my class to see how a problem-solving attitude overcame a real-life difficulty. By using a problem-solving response to any challenge or difficulty, it becomes a habit that can make the difference when resiliency is required.

Creative Problem Solving

Creative problem solving is to find unusual ideas and solutions that work. Do you think of yourself as capable of creative problem solving? Is that part of your self-identity? I hope so, because you have the same brain that inventors, artists, poets, novelists, song writers, and others use when doing creative thinking in their work. You may not use your brain for creative thinking as frequently as they do, but it is there for you to use. And the need for creative thinking certainly exists in today's world, because the churn of constant change requires you to act *and* think in ways new to you, and to have your new actions work well. When your new actions are effective, you are resilient. When you do not handle changed situations well, you are not resilient. It's that simple.

● ● ● ● ● ● ● ● ● ● ● ● ● ●

Dan Wilk felt frustrated. He was deeply committed to succeeding in his job as marketing representative for Opportunity, Inc., a Chicago area non-profit organization that obtains assembly work contracts for "handicapable" people, but an economic downturn was causing business to dry up. He did his best to bring in contracts, but had little success.

"There must be some way to keep our workers employed," Dan thought. "I wonder, if we don't have outside contracts, is there a product we could make and sell?" He started searching. He went to a wholesale supply showroom for office products and wandered around. At one exhibit he saw multicolored, rubber-band balls. He asked questions about how they were made. He learned that they were difficult to assemble by hand. At another exhibit in the showroom, a salesman showed him that new process had been developed for printing company names on wide rubber bands. Dan had an idea. "Maybe the workers at Opportunity, Inc. could make a rubber-band ball with an advertising message on an outside band that I could sell to corporations. But how can I make it easy to assemble the balls?"

Dan says he bought a box of multicolored rubber bands, a package of wide rubber-bands, and went to a toy store where he purchased a few Super Balls—a popular toy during the 1960s. At home, he and his wife assembled a prototype at their kitchen table using a Super Ball at the core. He wrote an advertising message in ink on the wide rubber band and showed it to potential buyers. His creation was an instant success. Dan applied for a design patent for what he called the Bandyball in January, 1993, and began to market it. He obtained huge orders from the Prentice-Hall publishing company and Walmart. The Eli Lilly pharmaceutical company contracted to use rubber-band balls with an advertising message to market a new medication. During the early-to-mid 1990s, close to 1 million Bandyballs were sold and distributed. Dan Wilk's creative solution to a problem that he was determined to solve kept many "handicapable" workers employed during a time when thousands of other people were unemployed.[7]

• • • • • • • • • • • • • •

One of the earliest recorded examples of creative problem solving traces back over 2,000 years to ancient Greece. In the year 287 BC, a Sicilian king had a beautiful crown of gold made for himself. But the king did not trust the goldsmith who made the crown. After it was made, he wanted to make sure it was pure gold, and that silver, a cheaper metal, had not been mixed in. The king asked Archimedes, a mathematician and physicist, to find a way to determine that the crown was pure gold without harming the crown in any way.

Archimedes was baffled by the problem. He tried many solutions in his home workshop but could not devise any scientific or mathematical ways to solve such a complex problem. Then one day, as he settled down into a public bath, he noticed that the water level rose. When he stood up to get out, the water level went down. Archimedes instantly realized how to solve the problem.

He was so excited, it is said, that he leapt up and ran

home naked shouting "Eureka! Eureka!"—which is Greek for "I have found it! I have found it!"

What Archimedes discovered was a principle in physics in which materials of different densities displace different amounts of water. The brilliant insight that excited Archimedes so much was simply that a kilogram of pure gold will displace a different amount of water than a kilogram of silver. Archimedes showed the king, by matching the weight of the crown against the amount of water it displaced, that it was, indeed, pure gold.[8]

You, too, can have "Aha!" experiences—especially when you need them the most. Your brain has much more information sloshing around in it than can be held in your conscious mind. Your conscious mind is like the tip of an iceberg poking out of a vast ocean rich with a lifetime of accumulated information. This is why people who can access the huge ocean of information in their brains are more resilient and more successful than people who restrict themselves to logical, rational thinking. Creative problem solving comes from knowing how to send insight-detecting probes through the immense reaches of your inner space.

An interesting paradox is that you increase your chances of having a creative solution come to you when you stop trying to solve the problem. Richard Wiseman, a psychology professor in England, is an expert on the differences between "lucky" and "unlucky" people. His research shows that people who feel lucky act in ways that increase their chances of having good luck. When wanting solutions or insights about problems, many lucky people will stop thinking about the problem, find a quiet place to relax, clear their minds, and meditate.[9]

Creative solutions cannot be found using logical, analytical problem solving. Creative problem solving starts with feeling that an unusual, new solution is possible. Then you ask yourself many questions to free your imagination from the restrictions of normal thinking and assumptions. You have probably heard the phrase "thinking outside of the box." It takes uncensored questions to break out of the invisible walls of socially approved thinking to let your imagination soar free.

A key component in creative thinking is an ability to make connections between remote ideas. To test yourself, here is a short version of the Remote Associations Test (RAT) developed by professor Sarnoff Mednick.[10] What is a word that these three words have in common?

truck   second   hired

A word that all three have in common is "hand", i.e., hand truck, secondhand, and hired hand.

Now find the connecting word for the sets of three words below. (The answers are at the end of this chapter.)

1. make   stack   seed
2. gun   pot   pool
3. hooky   double   mate
4. trial   night   guard
5. dream   down   water

Think of a situation where rational problem solving hasn't worked. It may be a situation where something isn't working right and you feel stymied trying to find a solution. The following suggestions show how to engage in problem solving that requires a creative solution:

+ Let yourself become preoccupied with wanting to understand all the details about what is happening. Saturate your mind with information. Be a curious observer.

+ Be playful in imagining various things you might do. Allow yourself some private, outrageous thoughts unfettered by judgmental thinking. The most creative breakthroughs often come after some far-out thinking.

+ Ask yourself lots of questions to explore the rich trove of possible solutions your mind can access. You might ask:

  ✧ What would be a different way of looking at this?
  ✧ What if I were to do the opposite of what I've been doing?
  ✧ What would be an outrageous solution?

⬩ What is amusing about this?

⬩ Is there a unique way to handle this?

✦ You can help creative solutions come to you in a number of ways. Get a pad of paper and start listing many possible solutions. Once started, open up to a wide range of unusual ideas. Open up to new possibilities by asking, "What if...?" For example, "What if I do the opposite of what people expect me to do?"

A technique called "mind-mapping" by Tony Buzan, is to get a blank piece of paper and draw a map of ideas. Place the central problem, goal, or issue in the center of the page and then draw a web of how the various ideas relate to each other. This gives you a different perspective on how things relate to each other—in your mind.[11]

✦ Take breaks and leave your mind alone. Go for a brisk outdoor walk. Detach and do not think about the problem; focus on anything else.

✦ Creative problem solving can be helped by relaxing and listening to music that has a pleasant effect on you. Listening to radio news broadcasts, on the other hand, can interfere.

Notice that one aspect of creative questioning is to ask uncensored questions. Psychologists have found that the least creative people think in judgmental ways. To be judgmental is to declare that certain thoughts and feelings are right or wrong, good or bad. This kind of internal censorship is a barrier to creative thinking. Self-censorship shows up in such statements as "That's a stupid idea," or "I don't want anyone to think I'm foolish," or "It's wrong to think this way."

In contrast, people who are skilled at being creative have a perceptual, observing way of looking at the world. They notice many things happening without judging what they see as right or wrong, good or bad.

An observing, perceiving person experiences the world with a silent mind. He or she is open-minded, or "open-brained." This person absorbs information about how things work just for the sake of knowing. Later, if a problem develops and a solution is needed, the person has a wide range of information to draw upon.

People with a judgmental style of thinking give negative labels to others—labels such as "perverts," "weirdos," "psychos," and such. They make statements such as, "Don't bother me with facts, my mind is already made up." Their minds are closed to learning about ideas that contradict what they think they know, closed to understanding people from backgrounds different than theirs.

Don't get me wrong, I'm not being judgmental about people who think in judgmental ways. Everyone is free to think and feel the way they wish, and clearly it is important to know the difference between right and wrong in human conduct. The point is simply that judgmental thinking can squelch creative thinking by crushing the seed of a new idea before it has a chance to sprout.

Closed-minded thinking is incompatible with creativity. One cannot be creative if facts, details, and information have never been absorbed in the first place. Closed-minded certainty suppresses curiosity. Ken Keyes, Jr., made almost the same point when he said, "You can't learn what you believe you already know."[12]

As you will see later, curiosity is an important quality at Level Four resiliency. You foster creativity by being a naïve, curious observer. You foster creativity by being like a curious child, filled with wonder about the world, not limited by opinions or judgments. To strengthen your ability to find creative solutions to problems, let yourself be curious, playful, open-minded, and awed in the way that you were as a child.

In fact, a child might see a solution that adults cannot. You may have heard the story about a tall truck getting wedged under a highway overpass. Engineers called in to assess the situation decided that winching the truck out could damage the overpass. As plans were being made to unload the truck and cut the top off with cutting torches, a boy watching everything asked one of the engineers, "Why don't you just let the air out of the tires?"

Practical Problem Solving

Sternberg's research group finds that children in some cultures are higher in practical intelligence than in the IQ kinds of intelligence that predicts success in school. Many people without a college education are successful in life because they are very practical in how they handle the world they live in.

A high IQ does not guarantee practical problem solving. A member of MENSA, an association for people with exceptionally high IQs, stopped at a tavern in a rural area late one afternoon to eat and relax for a while. When he came out later in the evening, he discovered that someone had stolen one wheel and its lug nuts from his sports car. He was distraught. He did not have emergency road service coverage, and there were no garages or tire shops open that he could contact.

A farmer walking by asked him what his problem was. The man explained, and the farmer asked if he had a good spare tire. He said that he did, but that the tire wouldn't do any good without lug nuts. The farmer said, "That's no problem." The farmer took the spare tire out of the trunk of the car, then used the lug-nut wrench to remove one lug nut from the three other tires. He used the three lug nuts to mount the spare tire on the wheel. He told the Mensan, "That'll do 'til you get back to the city, but drive slow."[13]

Many people have an amazing practical intelligence with "things." Farmers and ranchers are known for their ability to keep farm equipment running using baling wire and duct tape. In many large office buildings, the chief of building operations—the person who knows how to keep everything running—is not a college graduate.

The advantage of focusing on the problem and looking for a practical solution, instead of reacting emotionally, is well illustrated in this example told to me by Fred, a specialist in designing electronic testing equipment. Fred had worked for a large high-tech company for many years. One year the company had a huge loss of revenue. The president ordered all divisions to lay off twenty percent of their employees. Fred's job was put on the list.

Most of the long-time employees felt outraged. A good severance package and outplacement services did not keep morale from dropping. Fred sat back and looked at the situation from the company's point of view. He saw that he had specialized skills essential to the completion of an important new product that would increase the company's revenue in the future.

He asked around and heard that the company would be hiring a few consultants for essential work. He decided to try an unusual way to remain employed. He went to the company's employment office and presented them with his qualifications for being a consultant to his old department. His division manager wanted to keep Fred working on the project and approved his application. The company hired Fred as a consultant to replace himself—at a higher rate of pay than he had been getting—and he did not lose one day of work.

Fred told me that a year later, the accounting office determined that the company would save money by hiring him as an employee instead of paying his consultant fees. He laughed and said, "I went from being an employee to a consultant to an employee, and stayed at my same desk the entire time!"

The ability to invent a clever solution to a problem comes from wanting to find a good solution, thinking independently, and stepping outside the boundaries of old perceptions, assumptions, and habitual ways of thinking. It may also require having emotional independence from a group of people all hit with the same difficulties. The owner of the software programming company avoided getting swept up in group emotions and examined the big picture as an observer. Fred looked at the situation from the perspective of the corporate executives instead of regarding them as uncaring, inhumane villains—the way that many employees do during times of layoffs.

What we see here is an important prerequisite for problem solving real-life challenges. It's the ability to accept the reality of what's happening, without feeling emotionally distraught or furious about what others have done to shatter your life. The survivor personality research shows that individuals who survive extreme difficulties fully embrace what is happening. They do not decry or rage against what has happened.

If you argue with reality, you add to your difficulties. It's a fact of life that we become enmeshed in what we choose to fight against. You may not like what is happening, but the more that you struggle against it and argue with the new reality, the more trapped you become in helpless, energy-wasting activities. Arguing with a new reality is like punching a hole in the radiator of your car before starting a long drive on a hot day. The way to halt this kind of ineffective reaction is to pause and notice that you drain your energy during times when you think what is happening should not be happening.

Benefits from Good Problem-Solving Skills

All three kinds of problem solving—analytical, creative, and practical—may be combined when looking for ways to gain a competitive advantage in the business world. The owner of an independent automobile garage told me how he uses many kinds of problem solving to make his business successful. He said he looks for creative ways to provide better service than the automobile dealerships. He spends time imagining how, from the customer's perspective, his service could be different and better.

He said there can be a breakdown in communications when the service representative who does the intake writes the repair order. He eliminated much of that problem by having the service representative make a cassette tape recording of the customer describing the problem. Then, when the mechanic is ready to start work on the customer's car, he or she plays the tape and listens to the owner describe what the problem is.

In addition, if a customer does not have a cell phone, the garage owner saves precious time by providing the customer with an electronic beeper. When service has been completed, or if authorization is needed to repair an unexpected problem, his service manager sends a signal for the customer to call. They almost always call back immediately.

He analyzes his inventory and supply purchases regularly, looking for ways to cut costs and control his charges. The outcome is that his customers praise him for his outstanding service and lower charges—and they refer their friends to his business.

Practical problem solving is often needed in police work. One night, police officers chased a drug dealer into a large wooded area. They knew he was hiding somewhere in the dense trees and bushes. One of the officers radioed the dispatcher to obtain the man's cell phone number and call him. When the drug dealer's cell phone rang, the officers located him quickly.

This chapter covered three different problem-solving methods to develop. Look for an opportunity to apply and use them. Creative thinking can give you an advantage in any new or unexpected situation; use analytical thinking and logic to solve a problem in familiar settings. Your intention to handle life's challenges well can lead you to practical solutions.

When you follow the steps for effective problem solving, you not only solve problems better than most people, you develop self-confidence about your resiliency and sustain better health. The two-way connection between effective problem solving and your health works like this: When you live your life in a way that allows you to enjoy many pleasant moments, you increase your problem-solving strengths. When you cope well with various problems and challenges that you encounter, you enjoy good health and feel good about your life and work.

The key point to understand here is to think beyond any difficulty, problem, or adversity to your desired outcome. Build your plan on new or different actions you will take. A goal to get someone to stop doing something that you don't like or can't handle is not an effective strategy. Make certain that an effective solution to a problem will be based on positive actions you can take.

Problem solving can also be applied to the future. Is there a problem that you think might occur? Something that might happen, but may not? When you are skilled at problem solving, you can be ready with solutions for problems that might occur. You stay more relaxed and less anxious about potential problems if you work out Plan A, Plan B, and so forth—just in case something happens that you must cope with. In chapter 10 you will learn how this way of thinking ahead will pay off for you.

This May Be Enough

You can handle life's many challenges quite well with Level One and Level Two resiliency skills. You can have a long, healthy, good life by developing a health-sustaining lifestyle and being good at solving problems you encounter.

If you want to develop stronger, deeper, and better resiliency skills, however, there is much more to learn and overcome. Your progress to higher-level skills can be blocked by old mental and emotional habits from childhood. The next chapter, about the third level of resiliency, will focus inward on three psychological aspects of yourself that must be consciously developed and strengthened if you want to reach higher levels of resiliency.

Resiliency Development Activities

1. Reflect on what you learned in this chapter. Is there one kind of problem solving you use more than the others?

2. You probably have a sense of the three different kinds of intelligence: analytical, creative, and practical. If you had to create a team of three people to first create an important new product, then help you personally deliver it to a buyer in a country where it is not safe for most people to travel, what kinds of intelligence would you want in the three people you would select, and what jobs would you give them?

3. If there's a problem you've been wrestling with, pause here to work on it using the steps outlined above. Identify what information you need, and develop several possible solutions.

 * Answers to the RAT test:
   1. hay   2. shoot   3. play   4. stand   5. pipe

Chapter Six

Strengthen Your
Three Inner Selfs

You are fifty-three years old. You've been a state employee for eight years working in the Department of Transportation. You do your job well. You participate when sent to training classes to learn new skills and new procedures. You always receive excellent performance evaluations. You get along well with your co-workers and lend a helping hand when they need it. Your work is mostly satisfying, and you don't complain like some do about the hassles that come with being a state employee.

The voters in your state pass a ballot measure cutting taxes and forcing a reduction in state jobs. The governor orders a ten percent reduction in the workforce in all departments. You feel distressed learning that even though you've been with the state for eight years, you have low seniority. Your job will be eliminated in four months even though the work you do is essential to the department.

You take a class on how to write a résumé and do a job interview. Technology companies are major employers, so you make an appointment to interview at a nearby Hewlett-Packard plant.

You hand the interviewer your résumé and ask for a list of job openings and job descriptions. The interviewer looks at you, puzzled. "You didn't go online, did you, to research our needs?" she asks. "Here at HP we stopped using job descriptions long ago. When a work team needs someone with certain skills, they post their needs at the company website. If you think you have the skills and competencies a team needs, then come and talk with me. If I believe you are qualified, I'll arrange for you to have an interview with the team. Since you are here today, tell me, what are your reliable strengths and skills?"

You don't know how to respond. You stammer, "I've always received excellent performance evaluations. I'm a good worker. Give me a job description and I'll do whatever you want."

She shakes her head. "You don't understand. We don't want employees who need to be told what to do. We need self-motivated team players who actively look for ways to make themselves useful to their team. You have to invent your own job every week, depending on what your team and the company needs. What are your best skills? What reliable competencies and strengths would you contribute to an HP work team?"

You feel like she's asking you to brag about yourself. You were raised never to brag or boast about yourself. Good people are not prideful. You walk away feeling disoriented and confused. What is happening?

• • • • • • • • • • • • • •

If you lost your job, could you avoid feeling a loss of self-esteem and identity? During rough times, do you expect that you will handle new circumstances well? If pressured by others to be unethical, do you have strong inner values that you follow?

Highly resilient people know they can count on themselves during rough times. They have inner strengths they know they can rely on. The question is, what is the source of their inner strength? What makes some people emotionally stronger than others? In contrast, why do some people cower when threatened or crumble under pressure? What makes the difference between people who are emotionally strong and those who are emotionally weak?

The differences stem from three core inner strengths essential to being resilient. These strengths begin to develop early in life.

As children play and have many different experiences, they gain a feeling of competence about doing certain things. Their actions may be athletic, learning words or numbers, or skills with computers or a musical instrument. Their competence leads to feelings of *self-confidence* when they anticipate their ability to succeed at certain things in the future.

During childhood we develop emotional opinions about others and about ourselves. How we feel about ourselves is called *self-esteem.* If other children at school called you bad names, maybe your mother or father told you to answer back, "Sticks and stones can break my bones, but words can never hurt me." When you did this, you were learning to protect your feelings about yourself by rejecting bad opinions of you held by others.

As we get older, we develop ideas about ourselves that create our *self-concept.* Who we think we are shapes our identity.[1]

Three Gatekeepers to Resiliency: Deep Mind/Body Connections

These three essential strengths—self-confidence, self-esteem, and self-concept—function like gatekeepers that control your access to higher-level resiliency abilities. If your three gatekeepers are strong, they will allow you to develop a wide range of talents, abilities, and strengths that blossom at the fourth level of resiliency. If they are weak or you do not work at developing them, they will undermine you.

Every action, feeling, and thought has a physiological component. Your three inner selves stem from the three major nervous systems in your body:

+ The somatic nervous system controls your physical actions and is the source of your self-confidence.

+ The autonomic nervous system governs your feelings and is the source of your self-esteem.

+ The central nervous system includes your brain, and is the source of your verbal, conceptual thinking. Your self-concept is your collection of thoughts about who and what you are.

When the three selves are strong, positive, and healthy, you can count on your ability to learn valuable life skills that will help you become more and more resilient. You can bounce back from job loss, divorce, disabling injury, and many other life adversities because you know these experiences are part of the process of life.

Let me assure you that I am not urging you to go to unhealthy extremes. What we are aiming for are optimum, healthy levels of self-confidence, self-esteem, and self-concept, not extremes. As illustrated in the graph below, people at either of the two extremes are difficult to be around; they drain energy from people and groups they associate with.

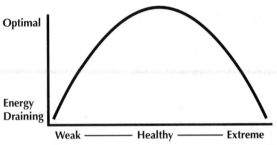

© 1993, 1996 Al Siebert

Once you develop strong inner selves and know how to replenish them if they become weakened, you always have them wherever you go, whenever you need them. Developing and sustaining these mind-body connections as part of your emotional lifestyle is similar to a team of athletes doing strength training before a competition: When you are tested by tough encounters, your team of inner strengths help you handle the challenges more capably.

When your inner selves are weak or undeveloped, you are vulnerable. You do not cope well with difficulties and are less resilient. Losing your job, getting divorced, losing your home, or becoming the target of false rumors may expose inner weaknesses that were not obvious in a safer, stable, protected environment.

During a workshop I was conducting for executives being outplaced, a pale, slender man in his fifties told me he was very upset about losing his executive position. With anguish on his face and a quiver in his voice, he showed me a business card and said, "I was the assistant director with a corner office on the top floor of my building. I used to manage over 800 employees. After they downsized our department, the director took my title away, told me I had a year to find a position someplace else, and moved me to a small office on the second floor."

He went on to say he was freed of all responsibilities and assigned a secretary so that he could devote all his time to looking for a new job. But he felt so devastated and outraged about losing his title and top-floor, corner office, he had made no effort during the year to find new employment. "What good would it do?" he said to me. "The people who left first got all the good jobs."

I felt compassion for this distraught, helpless man. He had been given a year at full pay with no responsibilities, an office, and a secretary. Yet he was so emotionally devastated by losing the external proof of his worth as a person, he felt crushed. I did what I could in the workshop to get him to look at his strengths, but his identity was so shattered I did not expect that he would recover without professional help. After the workshop, I urged him to see a counselor in the Employee Assistance Program.

Counselors see many divorced women whose identity was to be "Mrs. So-and-So." It can be emotionally rough to try to find out who you are at a late age if your identity was based on being someone's spouse and you then lose that status.

Fortunately, your struggle to recover and bounce back from adversity can help you unlock dormant strengths you did not know you had. Your effort to cope with a life-disrupting change can push you into a transformational inner journey in which you discover new ways to increase your resiliency.

No one's childhood is ideal. Everyone has had some things happen that should not happen to a child, and some things do not happen that should have. But this is OK. We humans can heal from early emotional hurts and make up for missing experiences. As adults, we can free ourselves from childhood experiences that have tied us up emotionally.

In my work teaching people how to rebound from devastating experiences, I often find that when I take them through activities to build strong self-confidence, healthy self-esteem, and a positive self-concept, I encounter some predictable emotional barriers, which stem from being raised to be a "good girl" or a "good boy." A person raised to be a good child carries old parental prohibitions against self-appreciation and self-praise. As a consequence, efforts to strengthen self-confidence, self-esteem, and self-concept may require confronting old childhood instructions not to think or feel in certain ways.[2]

Most parents were simply trying to prevent their children from developing *extreme* levels of these feelings. Such concerns are legitimate, because people with excessive self-confidence, narcissistic self-love, and a highly inflated self-concept have many problems in life. They're likely to make bad decisions, have fewer friends, and not learn useful lessons after things go wrong.

What You Expect from Yourself

Self-confidence is an action predictor. It is your gatekeeper to effective action. Think of self-confidence as your reputation with yourself. People with strong self-confidence expect to succeed in new activities and overcome unknown adversities. People with weak self-confidence do not expect to handle new activities very well and feel anxious about unknown challenges.

Anxiety is fear of the unknown. Self-confidence counteracts feelings of anxiety and reduces a need for tranquilizing medications.

How about you? When given a new assignment at work, do you feel confident that you will learn how to do it well? When thrown into an unfamiliar situation where how you respond makes a difference, do you expect to cope well and succeed?

You need strong self-confidence in a world where you are constantly required to do things you have never done before. If you join a new work team, it is important that you can tell others what your strengths and abilities are. False modesty may be desirable at social functions, but not when other team members are relying on you.

We are undergoing a significant cultural shift that is disorienting many people. In the past, organizations tended to hire cooperative, obedient workers who could get along with others, follow instructions, and maintain the established systems and procedures. Large, unchanging organizations needed workers raised to be good children who would serve in caretaker roles.

In today's world, however, caretakers have become misfits. Lean, constantly changing organizations need employees who can adapt quickly and work without job descriptions. Ones who are self-reliant, change-proficient, self-motivated to learn new skills, and willing to take risks.

You weaken your feelings of confidence with statements such as "I can't do that," or "It's all over for me now." You strengthen your self-confidence when you succeed at reaching a goal and appreciate your achievement.

To strengthen your conscious feelings of self-confidence, write your answers to these questions: "What are my reliable strengths and abilities? What do I do well?" List anything that you've been complimented on. Be sure you include skills with people.

To increase your feelings of self-confidence, pick a goal you'd like to succeed at reaching that you feel is moderately challenging for you. Avoid goals that are too easy, too hard, or depend on other people's actions. Then make a complete commitment to reaching the goal and keep at it. Seek feedback as you progress and adjust your actions accordingly.

Self-confidence develops from being good at what you do and from reaching self-chosen goals that are meaningful for you. One of the first psychologists to observe how people develop competence, Robert White, described how confidence in your abilities is a natural outcome of allowing yourself to act on your inborn motivation to become skillful and effective at what you do. White explained that spontaneous, playful experimenting leads to personal competence and a feeling of efficacy.[3] Research shows that self-efficacy comes from learning how to control your actions in ways that lead to predictable results.[4]

How You Feel about Yourself

Self-esteem is your emotional opinion about yourself. It is the gatekeeper in control of how you feel about yourself. Healthy esteem for yourself helps you in many ways. Strong, healthy self-esteem serves like a protective, thick emotional blanket that buffers you from feeling hurt by harmful criticism. Self-esteem makes up the gap between compliments you receive from others and what you need to psychologically sustain yourself. Managers, for example, receive more criticism and less praise than they deserve. Wives and mothers seldom get as much praise from their husbands and children as they deserve. In order to sustain your feelings of self-worth, it is essential to develop the quiet inner ability to praise yourself for good things you've done when others do not.

Self-esteem determines how much you learn after something goes wrong. If you experience yourself in positive ways, you are more open to learn from your failures or negative feedback. If your self-esteem is weak or excessive, you aren't able to admit to a failure or mistake.

People with weak self-esteem are easily threatened and manipulated. Because they depend on others to supply their esteem needs, they feel afraid that people will not like them. They are the most difficult employees to give a performance evaluation to. When told there is a behavior that needs to improve, they react as though they have been accused of being a bad person. They become very defensive and try to destroy the message and the credibility of the messenger.

Those with poor self-esteem often use indirect ways to get compliments, then they dismiss compliments when they occur. Perception is a function of contrasts. People with weak self-esteem may try to build themselves up in the eyes of people they talk to by tearing other people down. (See chapter 9.) These kinds of behaviors tend to have an energy-draining effect on the people they associate with.

If you were raised to be a "good child" who tries to never do what "bad" children do, it is essential to free yourself from the fears of what others may think about you. Weak self-esteem makes you vulnerable to be controlled by others. Start paying attention to your self-talk. Do you criticize yourself? Call yourself names? If so, break that habit. Stop tearing yourself down. Negative feelings about yourself weaken your resiliency.

To increase your awareness of the importance of self-esteem, talk with someone about differences you've seen between people with low self-esteem, strong self-esteem, and extreme self-esteem. This helps clarify that no one is suggesting that you become an arrogant egomaniac who feels superior to others. A person with strong, healthy self-esteem lives in the pleasant, optimal zone between two extremes that don't work well.

When your self-esteem is strong and healthyn you can shrug off insensitive comments from others. Public-sector employees need strong self-esteem to emotionally withstand many negative opinions about them. In my workshops for federal, state, county, and city employees, I hear the same story over and over. Public employees encounter negative opinions everywhere—in the media, in contacts with the public, and in their private lives.

Imagine being a public employee at a social gathering. Most people you meet will be curious and friendly, but there will usually be someone who, upon hearing that you are a public employee, will draw back and react negatively. The narrowing of the person's eyes, tone of voice, and body language all communicate the message, "Oh, you're one of *them.* How disappointing." Sometimes the prejudiced person will launch into a lecture on what the government is doing wrong. It takes strong, healthy self-esteem and a positive self-concept not to be hurt or wounded by such criticisms.

How strong is your self-esteem? Here's a test. How do you react when someone gives you a compliment? Do you say thank you and enjoy the praise, or do you get anxious and point out something wrong with yourself?

To strengthen your self-esteem make a long list of positive feelings you have for yourself. List ways you appreciate and like yourself. From now on, become a staunch supporter of your worth and value. Honor yourself, even if others don't.

After you have created your list of positive feelings about yourself, the next step is to do something that may require great courage. Ask a close friend to listen while you talk about the positive feelings you have for yourself. Do this even if you feel awkward and embarrassed. Practice saying thank you when your friend joins in and compliments you.

Have fun with this! Enjoy liking and appreciating yourself.

Later, when we get to the paradoxical inner nature of highly resilient people, you will see that it is also important to be self-critical. For now, however, practice being able to praise, compliment, appreciate, and feel love for yourself.

Accepting a compliment is not a sign of pridefulness or an indicator that you think you are better than others. False modesty is an act that attempts to manipulate what others think of you. It is an act that highly conscious people can see through. A better way of responding is to say thank you when complimented and enjoy the moment.

At times when you aren't feeling too good about yourself, here's a way to bolster feeling appreciated. One day I complimented a friend on being one of the best listeners I know. She smiled as she enjoyed my appreciation of her ability. Then she reached for her personal organizer and said, "I'm going to add that to my compliments file!" She opened her organizer to a back page and started writing.

I asked her what she was doing. She said she writes down special compliments that people give her. Then at times when she's feeling down, she reads through the file to remind her of all the positive appreciation people have expressed.

Consider creating a compliments file for yourself. Keeping a record of compliments is like having a photo album that reminds you of wonderful places you have visited.

Who You Think You Are

Let's look now at your *self-concept*. This gatekeeper is strengthened or weakened by your ideas about yourself.

Is your self-concept based upon your job title, income level, physical attributes, age, educational level, the price and location of your home, the car you drive, or having important friends? If so, it means that your identity is rooted in external factors. This places you at risk of having a serious identity crisis if you lose any of these external anchors for your identity.

It may be tempting to think of one's self as an important noun, such as "doctor, professor, judge, CEO, or the state tennis champion." It's better for your identity, however, if you develop a descriptive self-concept that remains intact despite a change in your job title, role with others, income level, or physical prowess.

• • • • • • • • • • • • • • • •

Actor Christopher Reeve was known as the handsome star of the *Superman* films. In his private life he was an equestrian who enjoyed competing in jumping derbies. During a derby in 1995, his horse balked at one of the jumps. Unable to free his hands from the bridle, Reeve's 215-pound body rammed head down onto a jumping rail. The blow shattered the first two vertebrae in his neck. His body collapsed into a heap. He was paralyzed, unable to move or breathe.

His effort to create a new life and identity was filled with many difficult feelings to overcome. Feeling helpless was hard for him to adjust to. By age forty-two, Reeve had appeared in over thirty motion pictures, television productions, and many plays. His role as Superman made him an internationally acclaimed star. He had a bright future ahead, a good marriage, and happy family.

Did the accident destroy his future or ruin his family life? No. He and his family adapted to his condition and became closer than ever. He accepted an offer to direct a motion picture and did so well as the director, it was nominated for an Emmy.

In his book about his new life, he said he avoided feeling anger and self-pity so that his wife, Dana, and his children could turn to him for advice instead of holding back. "What kind of life would it be for Dana if I let myself go and just became a depressed hulk in a wheelchair?"[5]

Just living day to day took him extreme effort, but he succeeded because he knew that who he was as a person was not his body. The title of his book about his life after the accident is *Still Me.* In it, Reeve demonstrated how a person can be physically crippled in an accident and yet go on to find fulfilling new directions in life while remaining the person he or she is. His attitude, exemplified by "still me," shows what a strong inner identity he had.

● ● ● ● ● ● ● ● ● ● ● ● ● ●

We live in a world where how you are perceived by many people and organizations depends on whether or not you have a college degree. College students who purchase term papers and do the minimum to pass their courses seem to think that success in life will come from having a degree, not from the education being offered to them. Having the status of a college graduate is so important in the minds of many people, it has become easy to purchase a BA, MA, or PhD diploma from an Internet "diploma mill."

Successful people define themselves. As John Murphy points out in *Success Without a College Degree,* many successful people have a positive self-image not affected by what educational level they reached in school. A person with a strong, self-defined identity and self-confidence may be more successful in life than people who think that having a college degree will bring success.

As reported by Murphy, a survey by *Forbes* magazine found that sixty-three of the 400 wealthiest people in the United States do not have college degrees. These include Bill Gates, Steve Jobs, Ted Turner, Steven Spielberg, and many others who followed a nontraditional path in life. Ralph Lauren, Walter Cronkite, John Glenn, and former president Harry S Truman did not have college degrees.[6]

Hundreds of high school dropouts have the highest levels of professional, athletic, political, and financial achievement. The celebrity list of famous high school dropouts includes eighteen billionaires, ten Nobel Prize winners, fifty-four Oscar winners, and eight US Presidents—including George Washington and Abraham Lincoln.

The lack of a college degree can hold a person back only if he or she believes it will. At the end of World War II, John Mitchell was one of a few who survived the infamous Bataan Death March, was taken to Japan on the death ships, and became a POW laborer in Japan. He'd enlisted as a Marine straight out of high school. After he returned home and regained his health, he was hired to be an assistant in the mail room at US National Bank.

Mitchell did his job well and found ways to make his job more useful than what his job description called for. He kept being promoted to higher positions and took every class available to learn skills for doing his job well. When I first met him, he was a branch manager of the bank. In the years that followed, he was promoted again and again until he became president of US National Bank. This happened during the time that banks were working to make their credit cards universally acceptable. Mitchell's skills and abilities led to his becoming president of the national VISA card association—an outstanding accomplishment for anyone, and especially for a man who never went to college.[7]

Throughout his career in banking, Mitchell never diminished himself or held himself back from an opportunity for advancement because he was concerned about not having a college education. Negative self-talk will weaken your self-concept and can lead to a self-fulfilling prophecy. People who think "I'm a loser" or "I'm failure as a manager" tend to act in ways that confirm those beliefs. People who think "I'm adaptable" or "I'm a good friend" will tend to act in ways to confirm those beliefs.

People with social or physical stigmas often develop a negative identity because most people they have contact with project a negative identity onto them.[8] Dave Pendlum was born with a cleft lip and cleft palate. Corrective surgery was not available to him in the rural foothills of Kentucky where his family lived. When he entered school, his facial disfigurement and severe speech impediment caused other children to stare, taunt, and mock him. He felt like victim and wallowed in self-pity.

Years later, after many corrective surgeries and intensive

speech therapy, Dave's life did not improve much. It wasn't until he was confronted by a friend that he saw he was still enmeshed in his victim identity. He set out to create a positive identity for himself. It was a long, difficult struggle for him, but worth the effort. His life improved in ways he never dreamed possible, and he has achieved outstanding career success as a senior government administrator.[9]

Psychology studies show a direct connection between the structure of a person's self-concept, their self-esteem, and how they respond to failure. Psychologist Carol Dweck and her colleagues find that self-esteem is vulnerable when people have a self-concept based on believing that their abilities are inborn—as something they either have or don't have. Dweck describes people who view their personal abilities as fixed aspects of their identity as having an "entity" theory about their abilities. Her research shows that such people experience weakened self-esteem after failing at something where they expected to do well.

In contrast, she finds that if people have an identity based on learning useful lessons after not succeeding at something important to them, they experience little loss of self-esteem after a failure. Dweck describes these people as having an "incremental" theory about their abilities.[10]

These two differences in self-concept have a powerful effect on how a person reacts to failure. Research with students shows that those who think a person either has abilities or they don't, fall into a helpless pattern after failure. Students who believe that abilities are learned and acquired, however, understand and accept that a failure is part of their learning process. Carol Dweck and Lisa Storich report that such students "respond with a mastery-oriented pattern after failure. These students remain focused and effective. Instead of doubting their competence, they take action to surmount the problem."[11]

Resiliency after a setback or failure comes from how you respond, not from your social status or social roles. Healthy self-esteem, strong self-confidence, and a positive self-concept develop in small steps over a period of time. You may have relapses when old feelings and concerns reappear, but new and better habits will gradually replace them.

To clarify and strengthen your self-concept, make two lists. On each list answer the statement "I am…" ten or more times.

In the first list write statements based on social status, job title, age, religious affiliation, education, ethnic roots, marital relationship, officer title in a club or group, and so forth.

In the second list write statements describing your inner attributes, values, principles for living, highest goals, coping skills, talents, and so forth. Include statements about your best problem-solving style, and statements such as "I am resilient," "I am able to handle pressure well," and "I am able to learn useful lessons from failures."

How Your Three Selfs Let You Be Effective Without a Job Description

In resiliency workshops, I usually ask how many people have a complete, up-to-date job description. Most people laugh; a few people may raise their hands. An ability to be guided by an inner sense of professionalism is essential in today's workplace. Many people think that being professional is an athlete who plays their sport for money or is a condition bestowed when a person has a graduate degree in a profession such as law, engineering, or nursing. Anyone at any job level can develop inner attitudes of professionalism, however. Individuals with a self-concept of professionalism quickly find new ways to be useful, adapt rapidly, are self-motivated to learn new skills, and so forth.

Lieutenant Commander Kenneth Cuyler sat in on a resiliency workshop I conducted for US Navy civil service workers. He participated in discussions and made comments that were well-received by the group. During a break following a discussion of what it means to work with an attitude of professionalism, he showed me a page in the back of his personal organizer. The page was titled "What Makes a Professional." He showed me his own private list of seven statements about professionalism. His list fit so well with what the class had been discussing, we duplicated copies for the entire group, and when our class resumed, I had Cuyler lead a discussion about the seven items. (During the workshop, I observed that the group held Cuyler in high esteem. Afterward, several of the senior workers told me that he was the best navy officer they'd ever worked for.) After our discussion, I urged the participants to model themselves after Cuyler—to each compile their own personally meaningful description of professionalism.[12]

Developing an attitude of professionalism about your work helps show that resiliency is not a new way of acting designed to replace an old act. The good-child syndrome means you try to act as a person *should*. In contrast, highly resilient people conduct themselves according to the effects of what they *do*. Resiliency comes from a discovered self, not a constructed self. It comes from the gradual emergence of your unique, inborn abilities in a process called individuation. The better you become, the more unique you become as an individual—and it never ends.

If your identity is based mostly on external factors, you will feel anxious about change that threatens your identity sources. You will try to keep the world around you frozen in place. If your identity is based on your personal qualities, abilities, and values, you can let parts of your world dissolve away without feeling threats to your existence. With a strong inner sense of who you are, you can easily adapt to and thrive in new environments.

When your three inner selfs are solid and strong, they can hold up well even when others try to weaken them. You have probably learned by now that there is no way of existing on this planet that won't be criticized by someone. A reality of life is that there will always be people who condemn you, call you bad names, try to tear you down, and tell you what you cannot accomplish. Strong gatekeepers protect you from such attacks, and let you move ahead with your life.

Strong inner selfs combine to create a powerful internal, protecting, stabilizing force. People skilled at resiling have inner strengths that can withstand many kinds of setbacks, even emotional attacks meant to harm them, without being traumatized or thrown off-balance. When they are hurt, they heal, and bounce back stronger than before.

● ● ● ● ● ● ● ● ● ● ● ● ● ● ●

Two organizational development specialists (I'll call them Stephanie and Priscilla) were shocked when the new deputy administrator in their state agency called them into his office and said their jobs had been eliminated. He said they would be transferred to another agency in a few weeks.

Back in their office, they felt outraged, hurt, and bewildered. They were known to be two of the best, most productive organizational development (OD) specialists in state government. They were skilled at systems analysis, strategic planning, process redesign, process improvement, and implementing transition and change. Through years of excellent work, they had streamlined many of the department's operations to high levels of efficiency and effectiveness. Their work was vital to internal operations and cultivating sustained capacity to achieve the organization's mission.

They knew there had been no mandate to reduce the workforce. The new administration had made a private decision, for political reasons, to eliminate their positions without consideration of merit, performance capacity, or commitment to achievement of agency outcomes. They stared at each other, feeling shock and dismay. A flood of questions welled up. What would happen with all their programs and the new mentoring program they had just started? Where were they going? What would they be doing? Would they be split up?

Co-workers rushed into their office to see if the rumor was true. People they'd worked with for years started crying. Many asked, "What will we do without you?" Co-workers at all levels telephoned and sent them cards and e-mails thanking and praising them.

After several days of turmoil, Stephanie and Priscilla agreed, "We really don't have a choice about whether this action is happening, but we do have choices about how we respond during this transition. We have to do this, and do it well."

They devised a strategy in which they would use their professional skills to manage the transition for themselves, their co-workers, and the work. They created a transition plan for leaving that they describe as including:

+ A period of emotional transition that we called "wallowing." We gave ourselves permission to cry, laugh, feel grumpy, eat comfort foods, be catty, make faces (with each other, not with others), and grieve what we would be losing. (Permission did not include trashing management.) We allowed ourselves several days of emotional wallowing, then ended it. We decided we'd be like redwood tree cones that need extreme heat to open and sprout. We decided that we intentionally would use the heat of the emotional fire to grow and rise, healthy and strong.

+ We wrote on the white board in our conference room all the wonderful things people were saying to us about our contributions and the quality of our work. Their praise was comforting while we were grieving losing jobs that we were so good at and emotionally invested in.

+ All the questions, "What will we do without you?" led us to a small epiphany. We saw that we had been catalysts at a time when our skills were needed, but that others could continue doing the same things after we left. Our transition plan included showing others how to continue the work. We compiled a notebook documenting all that we'd done. We did a lot of good stuff (and it was an impressive document to bring to our next position). We met with the people who had been active in our OD programs and coached them on how to continue without us. The notebook provided them with guidelines for keeping the programs going. We also gave them redwood cones that we collected from a tree near our building, to be symbolic of the phoenix spirit in all of us.

+ We identified the values that would sustain us through the transition and that we knew we would take with us wherever we would work. Our list included maintaining our integrity, cultivating/demonstrating grace during a situation that felt unjust, teaching, being good role models for collaboration and conflict resolution, using good communications skills, creating a vision of our highest goals, and constant personal and organizational improvement.

✦ We organized a going-away party for ourselves. It lasted all day long. It was a great event! Our month of facilitating our own transition in a graceful way paid off. People throughout the department felt confident, empowered, and optimistic about their future.

When the director of another department heard that Stephanie and Priscilla were available, she acted immediately to get them transferred to work for her. Stephanie says, "We came to our new department with ten products. We conducted interviews to determine which ones would be most useful right away and started with those. In the several years that followed we adapted the other system improvement strategies and got them going. The new department is twice the size of our old one. We have now developed many new products—some of them so successful they are being adopted statewide."

The resiliency shown by Stephanie and Priscilla when they were ripped away from their work and friends, came from strong feelings of self-confidence, healthy self-appreciation, and having identities based on their values and principles. Unlike many people who feel victimized by less disruptive events in their careers, they took hold of the situation and managed the process for both themselves and everyone affected. It is no surprise that they have both been promoted and continue to do valuable organizational development work.[13]

● ● ● ● ● ● ● ● ● ● ● ● ● ●

You've now learned how to master the first three levels of resiliency. In the first level, you learned what to do to achieve an optimum state of health and well-being. In the second level, you learned what to do to strengthen your problem-solving skills.

This third level of resiliency shows how three core inner selfs can weaken or strengthen your resiliency. They function like gatekeepers that control your access to fourth-level resiliency skills—the focus of the next four chapters.

Resiliency Development Activities

1. Think of ways that weak, strong, and extreme feelings of self-confidence and self-esteem affect the lives of people you know. If you know people handicapped by inner prohibitions from "good child" training, notice how they seem to be presenting an act to the world and how that keeps them from being resilient.

2. How much do "good-child" instructions from childhood control your life? Do you see how old restrictions against having certain thoughts and feelings might prevent you from developing resiliency skills? Are you able to speak easily with a close friend about your feelings of self-confidence, self-esteem, and positive self-concept?

3. To strengthen your ability to work without needing a written job description, list what someone in your line of work is like who has an attitude of professionalism. Contrast your description with your observations of people who act in unprofessional ways. Your inner knowledge about professionalism and unprofessionalism will help you navigate effectively through chaotic situations with an inner compass.

4. If you don't succeed at something, use the experience to learn a valuable lesson.

Chapter Seven

Unleash Your Curiosity: Enjoy Learning in the School of Life

My flight on the small commuter plane had only a few passengers, so it did not take long to board and settle into our seats. The flight attendant helped the mother sitting in front of me shorten and fasten the seat belt for her young, slender daughter.

During the lull before the attendant shut the cabin door, the little girl turned to her mother and asked in a loud, demanding voice, "What is cabin pressure? How can they lose it? If they lose cabin pressure, how do they find it? Mother, what is cabin pressure?" The mother looked at the girl but did not answer. Instead, she turned those of us sitting nearby, sighed loudly, and said with good-natured resignation, "It's like this all day long, every day."

We all smiled and chuckled. *Good mother!* I thought to myself, *You aren't trying to squelch your daughter's curiosity.* I knew that this little girl who wanted to know about an airplane's cabin pressure and how to find it when it is lost would become a much more resilient adult than children in classrooms being taught about atmospheric pressure on a day when the school curriculum has the topic scheduled.

I was impressed with the girl because our commuter flight would be at a low altitude. We would not be hearing any instructions about what to do in case of loss of cabin pressure. The girl had thought of her question by remembering instructions about loss of cabin pressure on a previous flight. (Later, after we were in the air, the mother had the attendant answer her daughter's questions.)

I was impressed with the mother, because a child asking lots of questions is not highly valued in many schools. Have you ever been to a high school graduation where a graduating senior was honored for being the best student in the class at asking questions? I expect not. I've asked that question to thousands of people in audiences all over North America and have never had one instance where an audience member indicated this was done at a graduation—even though asking good questions is a far more useful skill in today's world than knowing answers that someone taught you.

Asking questions is the self-motivated way a child learns about its world. A bright, active child asks endless questions. A child's curiosity is inborn; curiosity is not something that has to be taught.

More than any other species, we humans are born needing to learn how to survive in this world. Human children are not like insects and small animals born with preprogrammed neurology for finding food and shelter or avoiding danger and predators. "Lower" creatures have their brains hardwired, so to speak. The young can survive very soon without parental protection or help. But the more a creature's behavior is preprogrammed, the less its behavior can be altered through learning. The less preprogramming, the more a creature can alter its behavior through learning.

Needing to learn how to live in this world gives humans many choices. They can *find* safe environments, *create* environments that are safe for them, or *learn* how to survive in a new environment.

Curiosity is an inborn quality in all healthy children. Young human children are like adventurers who set out each day to discover and explore an amazing world. Children get into things, poke, bang, taste, and play with an unending array of new objects. Children crawl at first, then climb, learn to walk, and one day they discover they can run. It's an exciting time. As children learn to talk, their curiosity is expressed in questions. Asking "Why...?" goes on and on. In this manner, children learn about themselves and their environment, and develop competence for dealing effectively with their environment.

Rapid Reality Reading

Curiosity is essential to resiliency. Why? For a simple reason: If you are going to interact effectively with new situations, your brain must quickly acquire an accurate understanding of what is happening in your environment. Resiliency is increased when you quickly comprehend the unexpected new reality; it is decreased in people who don't comprehend the new reality.

Curiosity can be viewed as a sort of "open-brainedness." This open-brainedness does not distort new information with preexisting assumptions or beliefs. Active curiosity lets you orient yourself to new developments

People who have the best chance of handling new situations well are usually those with the best comprehension of what is occurring in the world around them. In contrast, people who have incorrect or distorted perceptions of what is happening in the world outside their bodies are not able to cope well and may not survive.

People with closed minds refuse to listen to information or feedback that they don't want to hear. It is not unusual for newspapers and magazines to run stories about how the executives of bankrupt corporations refused to listen to what their employees or customers tried to tell them.

In 1947, three scientists working in the Bell Labs at AT&T invented the transistor, a tiny electronic device that could replace the large glass tubes used in radios and would last longer. Transistors are now known to be one of the most important inventions of the 20th century. In 1956, the three scientists were awarded the Nobel Prize in physics for their work. But at the time, the executives at all the major US radio-manufacturing companies declared that the public would never accept transistorized radios. In Japan, however, executives with the Sony corporation saw the potential in the scientific breakthrough. They created a shirt-pocket-sized Sony transistor radio. Within a short time, US radio manufacturers lost most of the market for portable radios to the Japanese, all because corporate executives in the United States refused to be open-minded and adopt a new technology that US scientists had invented.[1]

When you listen to people talk about what they believe and perceive, it often becomes clear that beliefs they hold do not match up with what is happening in the world. They have inaccurate perceptions about events and refuse to listen to anything inconsistent with what they believe.

How about you? Have you ever refused to accept the truth about something? Have you ever had something go bad because you weren't paying attention to what was going on? Divorced men are notorious for having been surprised when informed that their marriage was over. Parents are often the last ones to accept that their children are doing drugs. An extreme example of denial was the time when a mental hospital in my state was being closed, but one of the custodians didn't accept that it was really happening until he showed up for work and found the front door chained shut.

▶ When you are hit with a major unexpected difficulty, get a pad of paper and write the Master Question at the top:

   ▷ What are the important questions I should be asking?

▶ Start listing questions such as
   ▷ What is happening? What is not happening?
   ▷ How serious is this?
   ▷ How much time do I have? How little?
   ▷ Must I do anything? Nothing?
   ▷ What are others doing? Not doing? Why not?
   ▷ Where do I fit in the scene?
   ▷ How are others reacting? What are their feelings?
   ▷ How do I appear in their eyes?
   ▷ What are others not noticing?

▶ Then search for answers as fast as you can. The more quickly you grasp the total reality of what is happening, the greater resiliency advantage you have. Curiosity links back to creative problem solving. Having lots of accurate information leads to creative, practical solutions to real-life problems.

If curiosity is a strong trait in you, you react to a surprising incident or unexpected development by wondering what is going on. An automatic openness to absorb new information epitomizes survivor resiliency. Curiosity is a valuable habit. Whether going for a walk or reacting to an emergency, you are open and alert to external circumstances, events, or developments.

The curiosity habit prepares you to read new realities rapidly. Your quick scan of a critical situation may include a fast reading of what other people are thinking, feeling, and doing. This ability to take in information rapidly is a form of high-speed learning.

Do you delight in being curious? Are you curious about the meanings of words, for example? I'm always amused when I ride in the back seat of my sister's car and see an old, paperback dictionary. She and her husband are the only people I know who carry a dictionary in their car in case they become curious about the meaning of a word.

The Fight for Your Mind

In the beginning, a child's life is filled with marvels. But for many children, their curiosity and active, self-managed learning becomes bothersome for parents and teachers who have their own agendas for children. A child may be told to stop interrupting with questions and to obediently learn what adults tell them to learn. The child's instinctive, self-motivation to learn is incompatible with the traditional training and socialization practices of our culture.

Educator Paulo Freire pointed out that societies and cultures maintain their identities, values, and beliefs by teaching them to their children. To this end they educate the next generation by telling them what to think, feel, and believe.

According to Freire, this process turns children into passive receptacles to be filled with the wisdom of the teachers. The more a teacher "fills the receptacles, the better the teacher he is. The more meekly the receptacles permit themselves to be filled, the better students they are."[2]

A student who wants acceptance and approval must cooperate and conform. When the training methods aren't successful with a child, the child is faulted. At the current time, it is a widespread practice for educators to declare that young students who don't passively cooperate with their teachers probably have an attention deficit disorder, and that the students must be medicated.

Freire saw that a teaching system that "domesticates" students inhibits creativity. This negates the kind of spontaneous inquiry that could lead them to discovering the world is not a permanent, fixed, static reality. He says a teaching method that presents problems and questions to students frees them to learn about reality for themselves in a world that is constantly shifting and transforming.

All societies come into existence under certain territorial, historical, social, and political circumstances. If those circumstances change, the society may be training its young people for an environment that is disappearing or no longer exists. The more a society programs or tries to hard-wire its children to think, feel, and act in specific ways, the more those children are kept at the level of unthinking, reflexive creatures. As a consequence, such a society is less able to adapt to new conditions than a group or culture that empowers young people to manage their self-motivated learning. Further, it is typical for a group or society run by adults, who were trained to think, feel, and act in certain ways aligned with past circumstances, to try to turn back the clock and return to the old ways.

Self-Managed Learning from Experience

People programmed to act, think, and feel in prescribed ways have little ability to learn from experience. They have *constructed* personalities. They have little resiliency when thrown into new situations because they react as they "should" according to instructions they were trained to follow.

While teaching resiliency workshops, I developed an understanding of why life is difficult for adults trained to be "good" children. They impose predetermined behaviors on situations, even when their actions are inappropriate and self-defeating. They don't know what to do outside the structured environments they were trained for. In a world of nonstop change, a forty-five-year-old person acting like a good five-year-old is as handicapped as an animal species unable to adapt when its environment changes.

Resilient people have *discovered* personalities. They never lose their curiosity about the world around them and keep learning from experience. They get better and better at handling new situations because they learn from the consequences of their actions. As workers, they are most receptive to performance evaluations because they want to know how to improve. They appreciate constructive criticism, and may thank others for feedback they don't like.

Fortunately, even though a person's self-motivation to learn valuable life competencies might have been suppressed early in life, the spark for learning can flame up again. The natural, inborn learning system that was suppressed can be reactivated, just as a computer can be rebooted after a software program freezes up.

Three Kinds of Learning

A marvelous blessing you carry inside you as a human being is that you can continue to learn how to cope, adapt, resile, and thrive in new circumstances *your entire life.* The famous psychologist Abraham Maslow said that no one achieves full self-actualization until at least the age of sixty. The key to enjoying this lifelong process is to appreciate and keep using your natural, self-motivated predisposition for learning new ways of doing things.

Level Four resiliency qualities blossom as we learn and grow from our experiences. A great benefit from being a human being is that we can replace old behaviors with new behaviors at any age.

It's useful to understand that you were born with the ability to learn in *three* different ways.

The first kind of learning is emphasized when students attend classes in school. What they learn is scheduled and controlled by teachers. School is a teaching environment. Teachers are evaluated on how well their students do on various tests.

A second kind of learning occurs from imitating effective people. From role models we acquire the action patterns of others.

The third way is self-motivated, self-managed learning. It is the learning that comes directly from your own experience. Life is a learning environment for people who learn on their own. In the school of life, a skilled student can learn useful lessons from rough experiences.

Here's another way to look at the differences in how people learn: When you take classes in a school, first you learn the lesson and then you take a test. In the school of life, first you take the test and then you learn a lesson.

Highly resilient people learn in all three ways. They learn in classes, learn from role models, and learn useful lessons on their own. A workplace reality is that employees who take classes on their own to learn useful, new, job-related skills increase their chances of surviving layoffs. When you learn ways to make yourself more valuable than your job description requires, you will be someone the senior managers want to keep.

Learning in the School of Life

How can you learn valuable lessons in the school of life? Here's an effective five-step process:

+ *Step One:* After having an important experience, replay it in your mind to be clear about what happened. (Remember: If you are upset, express your feelings to clear your emotions. Then return to the scene as an observer of yourself.)

+ *Step Two:* Describe the experience. Tell a friend or write about it in a journal. Be an observer of yourself and others. You do not learn when you justify your actions or criticize yourself. You do not learn when you get angry with others or criticize what they did. When you become an observer of yourself, you can develop choices about how to act differently.

+ *Step Three:* Ask yourself, "What can I learn from this? If such a thing were to happen again, what might I do differently or do the same the next time?"

+ *Step Four:* Imagine talking or acting in an effective way the next time.

+ *Step Five:* Mentally rehearse your better, more effective way. In your imagination, enjoy handling the situation really well the next time.

When you follow these five steps after something goes either well or poorly, you will handle similar situations much better in the future. When you encounter a similar situation again, instead of cowering, you will have positive coping energy ready for trying your new response.

● ● ● ● ● ● ● ● ● ● ● ● ● ●

Stacy Scholtz attributes her career success to being skillful at learning from experience. Stacy began working in management in 1989. Two years later she joined a large insurance company to become director of clinical operations. Over the years she received many promotions and is now a senior vice president. Stacy says her progress in the company came mostly from her way of learning how to become better and better. Her attitude is that every experience, successful and unsuccessful, offers a valuable opportunity to learn a good lesson. She describes her process this way:

"Here's how I've learned good management skills. For the last fifteen years I've served in various management capacities. I studied management concepts in graduate school, but the real learning was on the job. The process included

+ making mistakes, doing some things very well, and taking time to reflect on both
+ accepting criticism and feedback from mentors
+ trying new approaches
+ taking the best from some of my superiors, and learning from their worst

"I read management books and attend seminars, of course. The real expertise, however, comes not only from the years of experience, but also taking time to really reflect on what I've done well and what I've not done well and attempting to learn from both."[3]

An Antidote to the Victim Reaction

A learning response is the antidote to feeling like a helpless, mistreated, abused, beaten-up victim. When life deals you a rough blow, you have two choices. One is to learn a valuable lesson; the other is to remain a wounded victim.

The school of life arranges for many learning opportunities for people who react to difficulties by learning new skills and developing new strengths. In *The Road Less Traveled*, M. Scott Peck says, "Wise people learn not to dread, but actually to welcome problems."[4]

● ● ● ● ● ● ● ● ● ● ● ● ●

Actress Suzanne Somers reflects the kind of attitude toward adversity found in highly resilient people. Suzanne has overcome many difficulties. She had an alcoholic father. She married and divorced young, had a child who was injured and needed special medical care. After years of struggling to support the two of them, she got a good break and became one of the three stars on the hit television series *Three's Company*. When her contract came up for renewal, she demanded a raise. The producers decided to make an example of her for making such an outrageous request. They replaced her on the show and made it impossible for her to work in television or movies for many years.

In her book, *After the Fall*, Somers says, "It would have been easy to sit back and give up. It would have been easy to become the poor little victim. But then who would be the loser? This is my life! There is little to learn when all is going smoothly....But it is the pain of life's experiences that confuses us, depresses us, and tortures us so that we define ourselves and are forced to decide what to do about it. It is this frame of mind that helps us grow and evolve."

Somers rebuilt her career as a television star and says, "Everything that has happened to me has been a lesson. A wasted life is one in which lessons go unheeded. People who live such lives are the people who give up, who choose to be victims. I didn't give up. I am not a victim, and that is my proudest accomplishment."[5]

Learning from Failures

Experiences that feel like failures can break you down or be converted into growth experiences. Here is where the strengths of your three inner selfs play a critical role in determining which way your life progresses. They determine whether you feel devastated by a failure or convert it into a learning opportunity. If your self-confidence, self-esteem, and self-concept are weak, you interpret failure as a negative judgment about you and your incompetence. If your self-confidence, self-esteem, and self-concept are strong, you view a failure as feedback about the ineffectiveness of your current actions and as useful information about where to focus to become more effective.

Your inner response to failure is, at the adult level, something like differences in how parents admonish their children. Some parents say, "Look what you did. You're a bad boy. You upset me. If you ever do that again you'll be severely punished." Other parents say, "Why did a good boy like you do this bad thing? I feel upset. This is what I expect of you...." The difference is interpreting the failure as another sign that you are an ineffective person or seeing yourself as a usually capable person who did not handle this specific situation well.

A big resiliency breakthrough comes when you define resiliency as a learning opportunity. Charles Manz asserts that significant success in life "requires failure." In *The Power of Failure*, he says that if you would like to enjoy meaningful successes throughout your life, where you learn, grow, and have your life counts for something, "then you *must* fail. There is no exception to this rule."[6]

People skilled at learning from experience often learn more from failures than successes. Carol Hyatt and Linda Gottlieb say that when they started doing research for their book, *When Smart People Fail*, "We discovered a surprising fact: almost *everyone* we talked to, especially the most currently successful people, had experienced some major failure in their past." The interviews with successful people led them to describe successful people as "learners" and conclude that "it is the way you cope with failure that shapes you, not the failure itself."[7]

Ed Brodow has enjoyed many life successes as a US Marine Corps officer, television actor, chief corporate negotiator, author, speaker, and corporate consultant. Ed says he was raised by an uncle who was a lawyer. The uncle wanted Ed to also become a lawyer, so Ed applied to law school after completing college and was admitted. But he found law courses boring. He says, "I wanted to drop out, but the pressure from my family and friends was intimidating. The love they doled out to me was conditional on my succeeding." Ed acquiesced and stayed in school. Although he had passed the most difficult law school courses, twice he failed to pass the comparatively easy Family Law course. The dean told Ed to leave school.

"Getting kicked out of law school was a devastating blow to my ego at that time," Ed says. "I was relieved on some level, but the stigma attached to failure dogged me....However, this 'failure' actually marked the beginning of my authentic life. Everything I had attempted up to that point was based on my conditioning. After that, my mind and life were open to the field of infinite possibilities. In short, it was the best thing that ever happened to me."[8]

The Secret to Achieving High-Level Resiliency

How to achieve high-level resiliency is not a mystery. *The most resilient people are like children who never grew up.* A curious, playful spirit contributes directly to resiliency because playfulness and asking questions let you learn your way out of difficult circumstances.

When facing a challenging situation in life, the resiliency response usually starts with questions such as

- ✦ What's amusing about this?
- ✦ What am I learning that I didn't know before?
- ✦ How does this look from a different point of view?
- ✦ What would happen if I turned it upside down or inside out?

By playing and toying with a situation, you turn it into a game and avoid feeling overwhelmed. Laughing is an excellent sign that valuable real-life learning is occurring. An insight can be a delightful discovery and it can stay with you a long time.

Benefits of Curious, Playful Questioning

Learning in the school of life is what leads to becoming smarter, better, more change proficient, and resilient year after year. Learning from experience leads to practical knowledge about the relationships between events. If you do such and such, then certain outcomes usually occur. If, for example, you find something to laugh about in a difficult situation, then you have better energy for coping with whatever happens. Many of the guidelines for developing resiliency strengths are descriptions of "if...then," cause-and-effect relationships.

When you develop skills for learning in the school of life, you can

+ quickly find creatively effective ways to handle new situations
+ handle constant change without getting resiliency fatigue
+ gain useful lessons from bad experiences and look forward to future encounters
+ learn new ways to work or provide new services
+ build your self-confidence
+ avoid feeling anxious about change and unexpected challenges
+ get better and better every year at handling life's challenges
+ become more *you* year after year

Learning: The Key to Mastering Change

Introductory psychology textbooks define learning as "a change in behavior that results from experience." This means that change and learning are inseparable; they define each other. The key to mastering change is to manage your learning.

But learning skills are not enough for mastering change and bouncing back from adversity. As you will see in the next chapter, your expectations have a powerful effect on the outcomes of your efforts and your future circumstances.

Resiliency Development Activities

1. Reflect on what you've learned here. Think about the connection between curiosity and how it relates to mastering change quickly. If your curiosity was inhibited during childhood, coach yourself to become more actively curious.

2. Have you ever had a hunch or intuition about something, talked yourself out of it, and later wished that you hadn't? What did you learn from that experience about paying attention to your intuition?

3. Think back to an unpleasant experience in your past, such as poor work done by a repairman or a distressing incident with a neighbor. Search your memory for early clues you ignored. Use the five steps for learning from experience to learn a useful lesson. Write down what you will do or not do if there's a next time.

   Notice what effect the process has on you. When you replace negative experiences from the past with positive lessons learned, you increase your self-confidence, gain wisdom, and become more skilled at handling life-disrupting change.

4. Which kind of educational methods have you experienced? Were you conditioned to passively allow authorities to tell you what to believe, or were you challenged to take control of your own learning? What are your feelings about people who rebel against being trained to act, think, and feel in prescribed ways?

   How much does the following poem express your experiences in school?

School Child

What did you learn today, my child,
that you are loving and good?
Teacher says I need to learn
to do as children should.
And did you play and laugh
and run and feel your friends around?
The teacher says to please sit down
and not to make a sound.
How will I ever learn to BE,
how can that be taught,
when teacher keeps on teaching me to
to be who I am not?

–by Betty Esthelle[9]

5. What connection do you see between the way students are taught and the ability of a society to survive in a new environment? What moral issues are created when a group is determined to keep its belief system alive and intact, but the children must survive in a different cultural environment?

Chapter Eight

The Power of Positive Expectations

Primitive humans had difficult lives. Our distant ancestors felt vulnerable to many mysterious forces. In some years food was plentiful; in other years it was hard to find. In some years, severe storms, floods, and forest fires killed many people. Sometimes wounds caused people to die, but wounds sometimes healed. Some people recovered from sicknesses that killed others.

Our human brain gives us the ability to recall memories of the past and imagine the future. We can remember good and bad things that have happened to us and can anticipate good and bad things that might happen. People used their minds and developing language skills as best they could to try to understand and explain the causes of good and bad things that occurred.

Ancient Greeks believed that gods living in the heavens on Mount Olympus controlled the events affecting their lives. In Greek mythology, Pandora was blamed for opening a box that unleashed a multitude of harmful spirits that inflicted plagues, diseases, and illnesses on mankind. Spirits of greed, envy, hatred, mistrust, sorrow, anger, revenge, lust, and despair scattered far and wide looking for humans to torment. Inside the box, however, Pandora also discovered and released a healing spirit named Hope. Hope had the power to heal afflictions and illnesses caused by the malevolent spirits.

The Meaning and Benefits of Hope

From ancient times, people have recognized that a spirit of hope helps them bear times of great suffering, illnesses, disasters, loss, and pain. They learned that the spirit of hope could lead to being healed. And it makes sense. Now we know that positive feelings and support groups increase immune system functions and enhance healing. A wounded or sick person feeling hope could rest, be receptive to being tended by family, clan, or tribal members, and receptive to the healing effects of poultices, herbal teas, or medicines given by healers. Chewing white willow bark, for example, reduced fevers and decreased pain (the active ingredient is now manufactured and sold as aspirin).

The spirit of hope can pass from one human to another. The Christian *Bible* contains many accounts of early Christians being given hope or urged to feel hope. A compassionate writer, speaker, or singer can inspire (put the spirit of) hope in others. The name Hope has been given to towns, streets, community centers, and baby girls.

A person full of hope (i.e., is hopeful) feels less despair. Hopeful people endure longer, which can lead to healing, rescue, or the end of bad circumstances. Hope allows people to imagine that their present difficult life will be better in the future. People who lack hope cannot imagine a better future for themselves. To be "hope-less" is discouraging. Hopelessness portends bad future experiences. Hopeless people are likely to give up and not try to hold on.

Hope is meaningful when people are struggling to survive bad conditions. Without bad conditions, there is no need for hope other than hoping that good things will continue to happen and bad things will not occur again in the future. As long as humans experience diseases, tragedies, and disasters, they will also feel hope.

The Rise of Optimism

Gottfried Leibniz, a famous philosopher, mathematician, and inventor, wrestled with trying to resolve a widely debated dilemma: If "God the Creator" is all-powerful, all-knowing, and all-loving, then why did God create a world in which humans experience so much pain and suffering? How could a perfect God create what humans see as an imperfect world with evil in it? Leibniz reasoned that because God is the supreme, perfect being, God must have created an optimum universe—a universe with the highest possible degree of perfection.

Leibniz used the Latin word "optimus" in 1710 to describe what he reasoned is God's perfect universe.[1] The Leibniz optimus view of the world soon came to be known as a philosophy of optimism. Others disagreed with Leibniz and developed a philosophy of pessimism (derived from the Latin word "pessimus," meaning "worst"). Philosophical pessimism expects the eventual triumph of evil over good, world decay, and destruction. Philosophical optimism predicts triumph of good over evil, an improved world, and a better life for all. The structure of our language led to the creation of the nouns "optimist" and "pessimist" for people holding these opposing beliefs.

Hope, Optimism, and Self-Reliance

In their earliest forms, both optimism and pessimism were philosophic observations about good and bad things that happen in people's lives. These observations were influenced by widespread assumptions that the world functioned like a giant machine that had been created and set in motion by a divine hand and that humans were merely passengers along for the ride.

Humans slowly learned that their personal expectations, optimistic or pessimistic, can influence what happens in their lives; they do not have to be like parts of a machine or leaves blown around by the wind. In 1841, Ralph Waldo Emerson awakened many people to their ability to take control of their lives in his famous essay on "Self-Reliance."[2] Emerson's writings led many people to discover that instead of being passengers passively riding along in a huge mechanism controlled by external forces, they could steer their life direction in ways they like.

Two leading researchers into optimism and pessimism,

Charles Carver and Michael Scheier, explain that "optimists are people who expect good things to happen to them; pessimists are people who expect bad things to happen to them."[3] *Believing* that good events will happen in your future is different than *hoping* that your current difficulties will get better in the future.

Optimism and pessimism both tend to be self-fulfilling prophecies. If you expect a good outcome, your brain spots little events and momentary opportunities that can lead to that outcome. If you expect a bad outcome, your brain will have you thinking, feeling, and acting in ways that lead to that predicted outcome.

Psychologist Richard Wiseman finds that people who feel lucky actually are measurably more "lucky" than people who feel unlucky. He finds that repeated good or bad luck are influenced by what a person expects. People who believe they are lucky notice and act upon lucky opportunities, while people who believe they are unlucky notice and allow themselves to be defeated by unlucky events.[4]

Feelings of hope are tied to specific, immediate difficulties, while optimism and pessimism tend to be global expectations about things happening in the future. Jerome Groopman, MD, author of *The Anatomy of Hope*, said in an interview, "A person who has true hope will still have fears and will run through the gamut of emotions. A hopeful person also understands that things may not work out for the best, but they have the courage and the resilience to try to move forward through all of the difficulties. That's the way real life works."

He cautions that "having hope won't necessarily beat the odds, but without hope you are lost. Without hope you have no direction to go in. You have no courage and no resilience. Hope gives you a chance."

Groopman says that, as a surgeon, he has found that "an optimist believes everything is going to work out for the best. In fact, in life, that is often not the case. True hope is clear-eyed. It does not make that assumption. It sees all of the problems, all of the difficulties that lie ahead, and through those obstacles, it finds a possible realistic path to a better future."[5]

Optimism Strengthens Resilience

The terms "hopeful" or "optimistic" are less important than understanding that there is a connection between what you expect and do, and how well your life goes. Martin Seligman's early interest in optimism started when he became curious about experiments in which helplessness could not be taught to some laboratory animals or college students.[6] Learned helplessness could be instilled in many subjects, but not all. Seligman wondered, "Who gives up easily, and who never gives up? Clearly some people don't prevail, and some do."

He and his colleagues conducted research to find answers to these questions. "After seven years of experiments," Seligman said, "it was clear to us that the remarkable attribute of resilience in the face of defeat need not remain a mystery. It was not an inborn trait; it could be acquired." Seligman's "learned helplessness" and "learned optimism" research established that a way of explaining events that keeps a person feeling helpless, can be replaced with an "explanatory style," which empowers them and strengthens their resiliency during times of adversity.

Evidence is solid that optimistic and pessimistic beliefs affect people's lives. Psychologists Christopher Peterson and Edward Chang reviewed many research studies and concluded that "optimism, however measured, is linked to desirable characteristics—happiness, perseverance, achievement, and health—[while] pessimism is associated with undesirable characteristics such as unhappiness, poor health, and not trying to cope with difficulties."[7]

I should also point out that extreme feelings of pessimism and optimism are being emphasized here to make the importance of certain personal beliefs about adversity easier to understand. Many people are in the middle and are influenced by the mood of the groups they are part of.

When times are good, most people feel pretty good about their lives and their circumstances. They pay their bills, can eat out when they wish, and might buy a new car. When the future looks good, an optimistic person seems like most other people, but the intrinsically pessimistic person is made visible by his or her creative negativity. They can make negative predictions about any circumstance.

When times are bad, a pessimistic person blends in with the crowd. Thousands of people are out of work, don't have good medical coverage, have financial difficulties, worry about paying their rent or mortgage, and see little hope for improvement in the immediate future. It is during the worst times that an intrinsically optimistic person is made visible by his or her creative problem solving, positive expectations, and resiliency. These observations fit with findings by Carver and Scheier that some people have a broad "dispositional" optimism about life in general, while others feel optimistic about specific situations.[8]

Humans Have Attitudes!

Effective business executives search for ways to improve their operations and their products. This means replacing old equipment and production methods with better equipment and new methods. In the 1920s, some executives encountering resistance to change in their employees turned to the new science of psychology for help. George Mead and other social psychologists began studying the nature of attitudes in employees.[9]

Mead said that in humans an attitude is a predisposition to react with a fixed way of feeling and thinking. It is a form of prejudice that can be either positive or negative about almost anything. Research into the development, purposes, and functions of attitudes led to the finding that attitudes reach deeply into a person's identity. Children tend to adopt their parents' attitudes, and the attitudes they express determine acceptance or rejection by friends and other groups. Once developed, attitudes are resistant to change, because attempts to change someone's attitude strike at a person's sense of self and can stir fears of being rejected by those important to them.

About 200 years after Leibniz first developed the "optimus" philosophy, descriptions of people as having optimistic or pessimistic philosophies were replaced by references to people as having optimistic or pessimistic attitudes. Psychology research showed that attitudes are learned, not inborn.

Old notions of a successful person being blessed by the gods or born under a lucky star were replaced by a new understanding that a person from any background could become successful in life by developing positive attitudes. Positive attitudes became a new way to explain why some people who start with little in life are able to become extremely successful.

Almost anyone could control his or her own fate, it was believed, if they had the right attitude. People did not have to be passive pawns in the game of life. While hope and optimism were mostly passive conditions of waiting for things to become better, positive attitudes could energize goal-oriented action. The pendulum swung to the personal-action side. A whole industry of preachers preaching about positive mental attitudes and the power of positive thinking sprang up. "What you can conceive and believe, you can achieve!" is a common declaration.[10]

A Flaw in PMA Preachings

The term "positive attitude" is a widely used term in our popular culture, but is not a useful concept in psychology. Here's why.

A sales manager trying to stir a room full of sales people into enthusiastic action by exhorting them to have a positive mental attitude (PMA) is poorly informed about attitudes and how people develop them. Motivational speakers who urge people to acquire a PMA set many people up to experience failure, because repetition of positive thoughts alone seldom brings the promised success. Attitudes, as understood by psychologists, are not only mental. Most psychology textbooks define an attitude as having three components: cognitive, emotional, and behavioral.

Most people preaching to others about why they should develop a PMA give personal examples that suggest they have a high internal locus of control belief system. They may say they were miserable, cranky failures in life, until they changed their attitude and became successful beyond their wildest dreams. Such preachers don't understand that they are often speaking to people with external locus of control attitudes and beliefs—people who believe that their fate is determined by outside forces. When such people repeat positive affirmations, it is because an expert or authority told them to.

An attitude is an interwoven combination of mental, emotional, and behavioral habits. An attitude is a person's habitual, reflexive way of thinking about, feeling toward, and reacting to something. A person's attitude cannot be replaced by telling him or her to change what to think, but by choosing to practice thinking in a different way, a person can change an attitude.

A related challenge is that associated emotions and actions must also be changed, as well as the attitudes of groups important to the person. Some people may be open to consider changing their way of thinking, but it might cause them to lose important friendships and acceptance by others if they do.

Leave My Attitude Alone!

We also have the issue of whether or not people want to cooperate in having their attitudes changed. Let's say the leader of a work team you are on takes you aside and says they have decided to make you change your negative attitude about the new software program the company just purchased into a positive one. Or maybe someone tells you he's going to make you change your attitude about a political party. What would your response be? Do you believe that anyone can make you change one of your attitudes if you don't want to cooperate? It isn't likely; no more than anyone can make another person stop smoking or swearing if they don't want to cooperate.

No one can talk another person into changing an attitude, no matter how hard one may try—as many sales managers, parents, and spouses know full well. It takes a long time to develop an attitude, and it takes conscious, applied personal effort to undo or change an attitude—as with any habit.

So, when it comes to the matter of attitudes, think "habits." Then you'll have a realistic understanding of what it takes for a person to change an attitude. He or she must want the change to occur, and as with any personal habit, the practiced effort will take many weeks or months before the new way becomes established. Old attitudes can be replaced with new ones if a person decides to make the change, believes change is possible, and will stick with the plan. The key question is, do you control your attitudes or do they control you?[11]

Along Came Coping

Psychologists looking for ways to help people survive stress began to investigate specific actions people could take to be less vulnerable. In the 1960s, Richard Lazarus introduced the concept of "coping" as being a person's ability to successfully handle constantly changing demands and difficulties. The Lazarus research showed that effective coping included mental, emotional, and behavioral efforts to capably manage circumstances that might, at first, exceed a person's coping abilities. C. R. Snyder, a leading authority on coping, praises Lazarus for emphasizing "coping as process-oriented, rather than trait-oriented, [as] interactive instead of automated,... and implies a developmental rather than a mastery model."[12]

Folk wisdom shows that there have always been individuals who learned excellent coping skills from difficulties they've been through. The saying, "Good sailors are not made on calm seas," is one of many indicating that people can be "made stronger at the broken places." Psychologists may have lagged behind, but new studies of hope, optimism, attitudes, coping, and resiliency have led to an improved understanding of how people endure and overcome difficult experiences.

Learned Resiliency: Drawing on All Ways of Thinking

Resiliency psychology is making good progress. In 2004, the American Psychological Association "Task Force for Resilience in Response to Terrorism" published a set of fact sheets for psychologists working with a variety of groups. In the fact sheet for psychologists working with adults, "resilience" is defined as "an interactive product of beliefs, attitudes, approaches, behaviors, and perhaps physiology that help people fare better during adversity and recover more quickly following it."[13]

Humans in the past did not understand that their optimistic or pessimistic beliefs created a self-fulfilling prophecy. We now know that humans tend to interact with the world in ways that confirm their beliefs, prejudices, and predictions. People with positive attitudes act in ways to get the good results they expect. They give positive explanations for setbacks and persevere in their efforts. People with negative attitudes accept setbacks as proof of what they expected and as an excuse for not working to make things turn out well. Almost everyone does this, but only a few people are conscious of the process.

Both hope and optimism can contribute to resiliency because they are future oriented. People who feel hopeful and optimistic increase their chances of bouncing back and may make things even better than before. Hope helps a person endure through difficult times, and optimism provides thoughts and images of things turning out well. Hope is what people have. Optimism is what people believe. Positive attitudes are usually linked to actions people can take, step by step, to get them from where they are to where they want to be. Coping is an interactive process, different for each individual, in which a person keeps learning how to be better at handling difficult physical, mental, and emotional challenges.

Resilient people can combine them all. Highly resilient people are imbued with a mixture of hope, optimism, positive attitudes, and an ability to imagine a desired condition in a way that motivates and guides their purposeful coping actions. Such people *expect* and *need* good outcomes, and often get them.

This is new territory to explore. One interaction that has to be studied more fully, however, is the way in which differences in external and internal locus of control affect hope, optimism, coping, positive thinking, and resiliency. Research will probably show that people with high external beliefs will rely more on hope and optimistic thinking, while people with high internal beliefs and attitudes will show more coping skills and resiliency.

In the meantime, we can appreciate that over the centuries humans have gained much understanding about how their beliefs and expectations affect their experiences in the world. Now it is possible to combine hope with optimism and positive attitudes. This mix provides people with deep resiliency for holding up under pressure, coping with setbacks, and sustaining good energy in constant change. Their healthy energy, curiosity, problem-solving skills, self-confidence, and self-reliance let them scan situations looking for opportunities to take effective action.

The discovery that the good life some people enjoy is not the result of gods smiling on them reflects how much we humans have learned about ourselves and our world since ancient times. Many circumstances can be shaped in ways that you can influence. Future events are rarely firmly fixed in place. Resilient people know that unfolding events are not totally predetermined. The world is more plastic; it is more malleable and shapable than most people think. That is why people with hope, optimism, positivity, and coping skills have an amazing ability to get good outcomes in situations that have other people thinking that there's no way they can survive and prevail.

Employee assistance programs (EAPs) are starting to offer resiliency training and resources to their client organizations. The EAPs, until now, have been mostly *reactive* to people needing professional assistance. Now, the EAPs are beginning to be *proactive* in teaching resiliency so that fewer employees need emergency help. Externally controlled people will always need outside help, of course, but inner-directed, self-motivated people appreciate and learn from information about how they can be resilient on their own.[14]

The starting point for resiliency often begins with asking questions such as, "How can I cope with this? What is still good in my life?" An amazing thing about your brain is that when you instruct it to look for something, it often finds it. We humans can have two different sets of feelings about our circumstances. It's not a matter of feeling one way or the other, as in feeling happy or unhappy. If you define the situation too narrowly and think of it only as devastating your life, then other aspects of your life that seem contrary to your mind set won't reach you. People who survive extreme tragedies do so because they look for counterbalancing positives in their lives.

· · · · · · · · · · · · · ·

Joanne Hill lost twelve family members in four years. Joanne says, "There came the time when heartaches descended upon me like the locusts of biblical times. First I lost my husband, then my brother, followed by my dear stepfather, my mom, aunt, two uncles, stepmother, cousin, foster son and his partner, and finally, my son, who died of a heart attack. Multiple other family crises plagued us through those four years as well. My mother had Alzheimer's, cancer surgery, and a broken hip. Everyone I loved seemed to need help."

Joanne says, "Concerned friends often asked me, 'How do you deal with all the grief, troubles, and sorrow? How do you do it?' I delved into that question through journaling, meditation, and prayer. I discovered that in every stormy time, I could find rainbows if I looked for them. Here are the seven rainbow remedies that pulled me through:

1. *Stop, Look, Listen, and Learn* is the remedy that helped me take refuge from the storm, prepare for renewal, and grow from the experience.

2. *Praise and Thanksgiving* is a powerful treatment to ease fear and anxiety.

3. *Accentuate the Positive* brings sunshine back into our lives, bringing us optimal emotional well-being.

4. *Power of Choice* is an empowering remedy that truly makes the difference between whether we survive and thrive or wither and die.

5. *Forgiveness* is a potent formula to heal loss and painful relationships.

6. *Helping Others Help Themselves* is the prescription that lets you reach out to others while maintaining self-preservation.

7. *Support Systems* keep us afloat when the floods and winds of stormy times seem impossible to withstand alone.

Joanne says, "Others may find other remedies that help.

For me, these were the rainbow remedies that led me through the blackest storm of my life."

Joanne Hill's optimistic spirit and intention to be resilient helped her survive deep grief over loss after loss. She knew that despite everything, she could still find many joys and blessings in her life.[15]

The Dawning of the Era of Resiliency

Hopefulness, optimism, positivity, and coping were forerunners of resiliency. For thousands of years, people benefited from hope. About 300 years ago, optimism was added as a consciously constructed mental process. In 1841, Ralph Waldo Emerson affected thousands of people with his writings about self-reliance. About 100 years ago, positive attitudes emerged as a relevant factor; about 60 years ago, coping skills began to be taught. Now, knowledge gained from the new science of resiliency psychology is available as well.

The findings are clear. We humans are born able to learn how to keep getting better and better at handling life's challenges. The most useful learning is self-motivated, continues throughout one's life, and comes from direct encounters with challenges.

Any way of being can become self-defeating, however, when taken to an extreme. Some people who start their own businesses become so possessed by positive thinking they won't quit when they should. They spend their retirement savings, lose their homes, bankrupt their families, and may ruin their marriages and their health by refusing to accept that their business is a failure.

We come now to the next Level Four resiliency skill. It is the ability to engage in both optimistic and pessimistic thinking at the same time. The ability to think in negative ways helps minimize the disadvantages of being too positive. The ability to think and feel both in one way and the opposite is the basis for the mental and emotional flexibility that is the hallmark of successfully resilient people—the subject of the next chapter.

Resiliency Development Activities

1. Compare the differences between someone you know who is always optimistic and someone who is consistently pessimistic. Look to see how different they are in beliefs about the permanence of their problems and their feelings about being able to do anything about their circumstances.

2. Arrange for an opportunity to discuss with others the differences between hope, optimism, and positive expectations. Discuss how each of these can contribute to resiliency.

3. How important are optimism and positive expectations to you? When you face an adversity, is your self-talk optimistic? Have positive expectations helped you through difficult times?

Chapter Nine

Integrating Your
Paradoxical Abilities

Why do some people achieve much more career success than others? David McClelland, a psychology professor at Harvard University, spent many years searching for answers to this question. McClelland was perplexed by evidence that a high IQ and a college education do not assure success in life. Many college graduates flounder in their careers while people with little education are very successful. Many members of MENSA, the society for people with high IQs, work without distinction in ordinary jobs.

McClelland used his research skills to develop a test that provided answers to his questions. In fact, he became so skilled with his test, he was able to accurately predict, twenty years into the future, which college students from a graduating class would achieve the most career success.[1]

McClelland found that successful people work to achieve personal goals; they are not motivated to achieve social indicators of success. Success, for them, is a feeling they enjoy when they reach their self-chosen goals. This means that to enjoy feelings of success you must set goals and then reach them. No goals, no feelings of success. If a goal is imposed on you by others—teachers, family, or bosses—you may receive praise and rewards for what you do, but will feel little personal success.

The goals you choose must have personal meaning for you. For example, successful goals for you might be to complete a charity-sponsored 10K walk or to run a profitable home-based business. Self-chosen goals are more motivating. People work with more energy and persistence to reach goals personally important to them than less personally important goals.

McClelland's research went beyond the importance of setting and reaching self-chosen goals, however. Through carefully controlled scientific research conducted on thousands of people in different cultures, McClelland found that he could predict a person's future from the way that he or she daydreams about the future. He consistently found four elements in imaginative stories told by people who achieve and enjoy the most success:

+ They daydream about how they would feel reaching a certain goal. A girl learning to play soccer may daydream about playing on the US Women's soccer team one day.

+ They pick moderately challenging goals.

+ They engage in both optimistic and pessimistic thinking about how easy and how difficult it will be to reach the goal. Plans include carefully monitoring their progress so they can make corrections if needed.

+ They seek advice from experienced people before making a commitment to achieve the goal.

When considering a new endeavor, the person most likely to succeed will daydream about the *feelings* of satisfaction and accomplishment that achieving a specific goal will bring. The *feeling of achievement* is the goal. That is why they pick what for them would be moderately challenging goals. A goal with a 50/50 chance of being reached creates a situation where their personal effort will determine success or failure. McClelland found that achievement-oriented people don't enjoy gambling. They don't get involved in activities where the outcome is determined mostly by chance.

McClelland's research shows that high achievers do not charge ahead with unbridled optimism. People most likely to succeed at what they set out to do will spend time trying to anticipate everything that could go wrong. Before making a commitment to a goal, successful people try to predict the

obstacles, difficulties, personal limitations, possible problems, and barriers. They find out what they can learn from
experts and experienced people. Then they devise ways to
avoid the problems and difficulties or be prepared in advance, should they occur.

Bosses who declare they want to hear only positive thinking about a new project set their organizations up for big
failures. This restrictive way of thinking, described as
"groupthink" by psychologist Irving Janis, suppresses the
kind of critical evaluation that can anticipate potential future
problems.[2] Sales people who restrict themselves only to positive thoughts are more likely to fall into emotional pits of
discouragement. In contrast, people most likely to succeed go
through phases where they seem to be as negative as any
person who is pessimistic all the time.

Can achievement thinking be learned?

Yes.

McClelland proved this in a carefully controlled research
project with businessmen in India. He selected India for his
research because of the country's caste system. In India, most
people believe their lives are controlled by external events
and their stations in life.

In the India project, McClelland proved that with two
weeks of daily practice, the businessmen could learn to tell
imaginative stories in the same ways that high achievers do.
During the two years that followed, the experimental group—
the ones who learned how to think with imagination like high
achievers—significantly outperformed a matched control
group in achieving business and career success.[3]

The key point to understand is that highly effective
people can engage in optimistic or pessimistic thinking *as
they choose to.* Highly effective people are not on a one-dimen-
sional continuum, with optimism at one end and pessimism
at the other. Highly effective people experience optimism and
pessimism as separate mental and emotional activities. They
can choose to use either one—or both.

A good analogy is the way that you use the hot and cold
water faucets at a sink with one spout. When you want a

drink of water, you can choose to turn on cold water and not allow any hot water into your glass. When you want to rinse a greasy pan, you can choose to turn on hot water without mixing in cold water. If you want to wash your hands, you can turn on both faucets and blend hot and cold water together. Similarly, when you reach the advanced levels of mental development and emotional intelligence found in highly resilient people, you can exercise inspiring optimism, practical pessimism, or a blend of both, just like you control the faucets on a sink.

A Disadvantage

There can be a price to pay, however. Some people you associate with may be bothered if you let them know you can be both optimistic and pessimistic. Have you ever been in a meeting where the leader wanted only positive thinking? Where it was risky to raise a question about something that might go wrong?

A challenge you face by being able to think in both positive and negative ways is that our culture has developed the consensus reality that a positive attitude is good and desirable while a negative attitude is bad and undesirable. As a consequence, *most people with positive attitudes have a negative attitude about people with negative attitudes!*

This can create a problem for people who know it is practical to think in both optimistic and pessimistic ways. In an organization with leaders who emphasize positive thinking, individuals who think ahead in both positive and negative ways are sometimes labeled "pessimists." A technology specialist in a workshop said, "My manager doesn't understand. I point out problems he's overlooking to make sure we succeed. But he calls me Mr. Negative and tries to avoid me."

It takes self-confidence and healthy self-esteem to withstand negative opinions toward you, if people you associate with always want you to be positive and never negative. There are many social pressures to think and feel in one way but not the other.

One of the lessons that can be freeing to learn is that it isn't *negativity* that is the problem. The problem is people who express negativity in ways that have an energy-draining, de-synergistic effect. They give negative thinking a bad reputation.

Unpleasant experiences with unproductive negativity and people stuck in pessimistic mind sets have led our culture to develop a prohibitionist mentality. Because some people cause problems for others with their energy-draining negativity, a cultural standard developed that a good person should never engage in any negativity of any kind at any time. This abolitionist cultural norm helps explain why, in the past, many people with advanced emotional complexity had to hide productive ways of being negative.

People committed to thinking only in positive and never in negative ways try to maintain and protect a simple, closed belief system. They refuse to allow into their minds any thoughts or ideas contrary to what they believe is the only way a person should think and feel. Their closed-mindedness limits them to a constricted way of thinking.

As shown in the drawing on the facing page, people who try always to be positive and never negative can't tolerate hearing others talk in negative ways. They waste much of their mental and emotional energy trying to neutralize or eliminate the negativity in others. This huge expenditure of time and mental and emotional energy accomplishes very little. They often feel stuck in a frustrating conflict with their upsetting opposite.

Three Ways of Being with Positive and Negative Thinking

When it comes to positive and negative, or optimistic and pessimistic, mental and emotional energies, people usually fit into one of three patterns:

1. A person can choose to think and feel in any positive and/or negative way, as called for.

2. Positivity and negativity specialists appreciate each other and create a cooperative working relationship.

3. Positive/not-negative specialists and negative/not-positive specialists invalidate each other and drain each other's energy.

LEVELS OF POSITIVE AND NEGATIVE THINKING

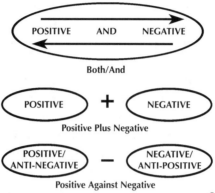

© 1993, 1996 Al Siebert

Where do you place yourself? Which is your usual level? The irony is that people who remain stuck at the lowest level often create the very situation they protest about. Here's how it works: A person who puts energy into being positive and not negative creates an emotional vacuum for negative thinking. Scientists know that nature fills a vacuum, and the same holds true here. A person who practices positive thinking only, will usually have a child, spouse, or co-worker who becomes more and more negative. Nature fills the vacuum, and the two parties drive each other crazy. Each protests to anyone who will listen, "If only that other person would change, my life would be much better."

A friend of mine says her mother was a devotee of Dr. Norman Vincent Peale, author of *The Power of Positive Thinking.* Her mother attended his church in New York City and became a paragon of positive thinking from morning until night. My friend says her reaction to her mother's constant positive thinking was to become more and more negative. After leaving home, it took her many years to overcome her negative mental habits.

What locks a positivity specialist into an unending struggle with negativity specialists is that this upsetting anti-model in their lives is a frame of reference for their good person identity. Thus, they can never succeed in changing the other person because they need the social contrast with a person they invalidate to show that they are good.

If positivity specialists reach a point of feeling too upset and worn out by more exposure to negative thinking than they think they can continue to deal with, they may or may not discover that they are at a choice point in life. If they consider the possibility that both the cause of their difficulty and the solution to it lies within themselves, they may make the growth choice by accepting responsibility for their reactions to people they feel upset by. The other option is to drift deeper into their draining struggle with negativity specialists.

People who strengthen their self-esteem and give up needing an invalidated anti-model as proof of how good they are experience deep emotional relief. Their energies are freed for more productive activities, and they may even appreciate benefits of having a negativity specialist in their lives.

We judge others by the effects of their actions, ourselves by our explanations. When you use empathy skills to validate people who act in ways that upset you, you can break free from feeling mired down by people who act in ways that you don't like.[4]

Free Your Mind from Labels for Others

Another mental and emotional barrier that locks people into the energy-draining, constricted level of thinking is to label people as being pessimists or optimists. Labeling is to think of people as nouns. Thinking of people as nouns, as "things," simplifies perceptions for the observer but limits comprehension. It's a child's way of thinking that prevents an accurate understanding of people who are complex and emotionally flexible.

This is partly a social problem because many psychologists refer to people as nouns. Researchers into optimism write about optimists and pessimists in their books and journals. In my college courses, I was taught ways that extroverts differ from introverts.

Most psychology personality tests categorize people as being either one type of person or another. At a professional gathering, a woman walked up to me, smiled, extended her hand to shake mine, and said, "Hi! I'm Sue. I'm an INTJ."

"Is that so?" I asked. "From the way you walked up to me I'd say you are acting like an ESFP right now."

Sue looked startled. Her hand went limp. "But according to the Myers-Briggs personality test," she said, "I'm an INTJ."

"That's its weakness," I said. "It tends to have people thinking of each other as clusters of initials. It doesn't validate and explain how to understand highly complex people who may be very high on each of the opposing dimensions. I think you are more complex and changeable from one situation to another than the test indicated."

My response to Sue was a sign of progress for me. In graduate school, I'd acquired a mind set that people are either one way or another. That's why highly resilient survivors puzzled me at first. In my interviews, I learned that the most resilient people are both extroverted *and* introverted, both thoughtful and outgoing, serious and humorous, hard-working and lazy, self-confident and self-critical. I found that on any dimension of personality, they are rarely one way *or* the other; they are usually *both* one way *and* the other.[5]

Highly Resilient People Have Many Counterbalanced Traits

The complex inner nature of highly resilient survivors made me wonder how their paradoxical personality traits were related to being resilient. I found an answer in the writings of T. C. Schneirla, a scientist famous for his studies of animal behavior. His research showed that for any creature to survive, it must be able to move toward food and safety, and away from danger. Professor Schneirla created the phrase "biphasic pattern of adjustment" to describe a creature's ability to approach or withdraw.[6]

Opposing muscular systems in our bodies make biphasic patterns of physical movement possible. We have precise control over our physical actions because flexor and extensor muscles work in counterbalanced opposition to each other. This counterbalanced control is like having both forward and reverse gears in a car. Without a reverse gear, a car can get stuck in places where forward progress is blocked. When I was a freshman in college, one of the seniors had an old Ford like that. Whenever he wanted to drive some place in town, he would take several freshmen along. He'd have them jump out and push his car backward whenever he needed to back up.

The same principles governing our physiology can usually be found in our minds and personalities. The equivalent of counterbalanced muscle systems are counterbalanced or paradoxical personality traits.

Abraham Maslow pointed out that highly self-actualized people go beyond acting in selfish and unselfish ways. He said they combine both selfishness and unselfishness into the same activity. An unselfish action to help an injured stranger, for example, *must* be done. To walk away would be unthinkable and emotionally distressing to live with. Maslow also observed that the emotional rewards from unselfish actions are a selfish benefit. Thus it is that helping others can be seen as motivated by "selfish unselfishness."[7]

Maslow's insight had a powerful effect on my thinking. I began to see many pairs of opposite traits combined in highly resilient people. The most resilient people seem to function with extroverted introversion, pessimistic optimism, selfish unselfishness, cooperative nonconformity, moral lust, playful seriousness, and more. Returning to the faucet analogy, the blended opposites in some people are like the single faucets installed in some kitchens and showers. One lever or knob gives you control over any mixture of hot and cold water you desire, and control over the volume as well.

People who think or feel in both one way and the opposite have counterbalanced traits. Once I broke through the mental barrier, it became fun to observe paradoxical qualities in people. One Saturday night, for example, I was at a party near the university campus. Most of the people were graduate students and faculty members. I was talking with a woman when she gestured toward a young man sitting by himself in the middle of the room with his head down. During the evening, he had rebuffed people's efforts to engage him in conversation. The woman said, "You're a psychologist; he's a real introvert, isn't he?"

I thought about her question for a moment, then said, "No."

She looked at me, perplexed. She said, "But look at him; he won't talk to anyone. He's so shy."

I said, "You are right about that, but notice that he's sitting in the middle of one of the noisiest parties near campus on a Saturday night. He's showing off his introversion in a very extroverted way. If he was truly an introvert, as you say, he would be drinking alone in his apartment."

She laughed, and we resumed our conversation—leaving the young man to remain conspicuously shy.

Paradoxical Complexity Increases Resiliency and Emotional Intelligence

Here is a list of the kinds of personality qualities usually observed in highly resilient survivors. Look through the list below to see how many of these pairs of counterbalanced qualities describe you:

creative and analytical
serious and playful
hard-working and lazy
sensitive and tough
cautious and trusting
unselfish and selfish
self-appreciating and self-critical
impulsive and thorough
stable and unpredictable
optimistic and pessimistic
outgoing and introspective

Additional pairs that describe you:

Counterbalanced personality qualities indicate that you have developed advanced emotional intelligence. The more *pairs* of traits you have, the more you have the mental and emotional flexibility essential for resiliency. If you added several pairs of qualities to the list, that's even better. The list is not meant to be complete. It can't be. Every human is more complex and has more dimensions than any list could fully cover.

Your agility in rapidly changing circumstances comes from having many such pairs of traits, whatever they may be. The benefits gained from having many, well-integrated, counterbalanced complexities is nicely demonstrated by rubber-band balls. One rubber band can't bounce off a floor by itself, but dozens of rubber bands wrapped together in mild, sustained tension have an amazing ability to bounce back.

The longer the list of pairs of paradoxical, counterbalanced, or biphasic traits you recognize in yourself, the more emotionally complex you are, and this can increase your chances of successfully handling any situation that develops. So, in this sense, you become predictable. The specific way that you will do something may not be predictable, but your ability to be agile and make things turn out well becomes more predictable.

Many people feel delighted when they hear that counterbalanced traits are signs of resiliency and advanced emotional intelligence. Some highly complex individuals say that their paradoxical nature has drawn negative reactions from others. A few people have privately thanked me after learning that they are not borderline schizophrenic, that it is emotionally healthy for them to have many opposite feelings.

It is essential that you feel comfortable having thoughts and feelings that seem inconsistent or contradictory. Here is another instance where you must have strong self-esteem and a strong sense of yourself so as not to be emotionally inhibited by people who can't handle exposure to paradoxical thoughts and feelings in others.

Having a variety of responses is crucial when handling unpredictable, chaotic, or changing conditions. Successful people in every profession know that it is better to have many possible responses than to be limited to a few. In martial arts, it is better to have many possible moves than be limited to only one or two. Bruce Lee achieved outstanding success in the martial arts because he developed a way of using no pre-set form when engaging opponents. He called it Wu-Wei, the way of no way. He allowed creative intuition to guide spontaneous action without taking designed, pre-planned action.[8]

Adaptation is the key to survival in all of nature. If you always respond one way and never in the opposite way, you will sometimes be helpless to stop yourself from automatically reacting and will do or say something that you later regret. A behavior that cannot be consciously stopped or reversed is not under control.

When someone does not handle life's challenges well, it is often because this person always thinks, feels, or acts in only one way and would never consider doing the opposite. Many people are so taken with the idea of being self-starting, for example, they lose sight of the need for the counterbalancing skill of being self-stopping. A real-estate salesman I knew said he could work long hours, day after day, but then would have days when he had no energy to do anything. I saw that he didn't know how to stop himself, take breaks, and rest. His body would protect itself and take control at a level stronger than his mental willpower.

A person who can act in only one way has little self-control and, therefore, must be kept in check by others. Have you ever known a person who didn't know when to stop talking? Such a person keeps going and will continue until the listener interrupts or ends the conversation. The less a person can stop or consciously reverse a behavior, the more that person's behavior will be controlled by external forces.

The old way of thinking, that one's personality traits should be constant in all situations, is very limiting. Don't handicap yourself by believing that you have to stick with one personality trait and never do the opposite. Many inner potentials can emerge when you allow yourself to respond to a situation, or to view it in any way that you choose.

You enjoy a better, more emotionally intelligent understanding of resilient people when you are open to experience their emotional complexity. If you are a good listener, you are likely to hear a resilient survivor describe that a disastrous experience had both negative and positive aspects.

●●●●●●●●●●●●●●

Larry Newman lost everything he owned in the 1987 earthquake that devastated southern California. "I was terrified," he says, "when the earthquake shook my apartment building. I'd just gotten out of bed when it hit. Electrical sparks were flying. The whole place was set ablaze. I knew I had to get out, and fast.

"Since I had no clothes on, I grabbed my bathrobe and ran outside. I stood there with neighbors watching fire pouring out of my windows, burning up everything I owned.

"As I watched, the impact of what was happening hit me, and my mind started to reel. Not only was my past melting before my eyes, but my future was less certain than ever. Over the previous year, I had been struggling as a non-union movie extra, aspiring to an acting career. But my income was so low I was unable to accumulate enough money to join the Screen Actor's Guild. Becoming a member would open doors for me, triple my income, and greatly further my career. Now my wardrobe, crucial for getting acting jobs, was turning to ashes.

"Two neighbors saw that I was wearing only my bathrobe. They took me to their home and gave me some clothes and shoes. I telephoned two of my dear friends, who welcomed me into their apartment with open arms, a bed, food, and love. After I settled in and let down, I started thinking about what would happen to me. My mind began racing with negative thoughts about my situation.

"But soon after, a great calm descended upon me—almost as if a giant hand was reining in a runaway horse. I realized that I was in one piece. All I had to do to stay on an even keel was to deal with one thing at a time, one moment at a time, one day at a time.

"Two days after the fire, I went to a Federal Emergency Management Agency office and filled out their forms. Two days later, a rep met me at my apartment to survey the damage. Within ten days of the fire I received a check for $5,000.

The money let me purchase a new wardrobe that was better than what I had before and allowed me to join the Screen Actor's Guild.

"Now when people ask me about the earthquake, I tell them it was a bad/good experience. The fire turned from a tragedy into a blessing, in both professional and personal ways. The fire strengthened my belief that things can be replaced and that the most important aspect of any event is how you react to it. My experience put me in empathetic touch with those who have suffered a similar experience. I am now regularly employed as an actor and wake each morning relishing the thought of going to work. Plus, all the emotions I experienced help me as an actor; the fire gave me a multitude of emotions to draw on.

"Upon reflection, it appears to me that life is full of positive surprises, and they usually come in the most unexpected ways. For anyone facing a similar situation, I would say to think of life as being in a small boat with your hand on the tiller. A major storm erupts and tosses you about, but if you keep a steady hand on the tiller, it is only a matter of time before the storm subsides and the sun breaks through."[9]

* * * * * * * * * * * * *

Counterbalanced Complexity Increases Mental and Emotional Strength

Counterbalanced or paradoxical personality traits are not signs of emotional instability. Just the opposite. Well-integrated inner complexities increase your psychological stability and give you greater mental and emotional flexibility for dealing with many circumstances.

In work teams, for example, a quickly adaptable person might assume informal leadership when things are in turmoil, or quietly follow along if things are running well. He or she might initiate creative brainstorming when the group is stuck, or be the conservative voice of caution if others are trying too many new ideas. If the group is overly optimistic, this person might add a pessimistic perspective, but then turn around and be optimistic if the group is too pessimistic. If you can be flexible in groups, that is a good sign.

If you try to think about yourself or others as being either one way or the opposite, you will place invisible restraints on your choices of responses and will not understand the flexible nature of highly resilient survivors very well. When you think of yourself and others as able to be both one way and the opposite, you free yourself to be more flexible and curious, not bothered, when others act in ways opposite from what you expect. This is why in the chapter on how to develop a strong self-concept, you were urged not to define your identity by your job title or role in a relationship, but to identify yourself by describing your personality traits, strengths, and ability to learn from not succeeding at something.

Every person is more complex and unique than any label. I have found that describing people's actions, feelings, and thoughts lets me see them and understand them with more clarity than can happen if I label them. As was stated above, labeling people as pessimists, optimists, liberals, extroverts, alcoholics, schizophrenics, perverts, or whatever, is simplistic, lacks emotional intelligence, and limits understanding.

Descriptive adjectives are useful. Notice that I describe people as having traits or abilities called optimism, extroversion, pessimism, and such. I do this in a way that allows myself to see that the person may also be exhibiting the opposite, counterbalancing trait. Describing what individuals actually say and do instead of labeling them is a valuable mental achievement. It is also an indication of advanced emotional intelligence. Psychologist Paul Wieand teaches executives how to develop advanced emotional intelligence in ways that include discovering and valuing their counterbalanced traits and feelings.[10]

Your own mix of counterbalanced qualities might confuse others, and even feel contradictory within yourself at times, but the ability to use both one way of thinking or feeling and its opposite can be of tremendous help in taking effective action at the right time. Tough problems may require you to use both logical reasoning *and* creative intuition, to be both serious *and* playful. Having a wide range of responses in unstable, chaotic, new situations increases your resiliency.

Three Ways of Being with Mental and Emotional Counterbalanced Dimensions

The same three patterns in the ways that humans express positive and negative thinking can be seen in every dimension of thinking and feeling that humans express. Here is how internal and external locus of control beliefs are expressed at the three levels:

1. *Counterbalanced:* Highly resilient, synergistic people can be both powerfully self-motivated (high internal locus of control) and also feel at ease being cooperatively compliant (high external locus of control.)

2. *Appreciating pairs:* Self-motivated individuals and people who prefer to be told what to do enjoy a good working relationship.

3. *Invalidating oppositional:* Fiercely self-motivated people have poor opinions about people who need to be told what to do, while people who wait to be told what to do resent people who order them around.

Here are the three levels as seen in the ways that people are task oriented and relationship oriented:

1. *Counterbalanced:* Highly resilient, synergistic people can focus both on tasks and relationships.

2. *Appreciating pairs:* Task-oriented people and those who emphasize relationships appreciate each other and enjoy good working partnerships.

3. *Invalidating oppositional:* Task-focused people invalidate "touchy-feely" relationship-oriented people whom they see as wasting valuable working time in personal conversations, while people who believe that relationships are more important than working, spend time gossiping about insensitive, work-driven people.

Choosing the Empowering Path

Once you understand the dynamics of the three levels, you can fill in any dimension on which humans differ at one level or another. Using the blank diagram below, think of people you've known who place at one of the three levels on these dimensions:

optimistic—pessimistic
self-motivated—unmotivated
task oriented—people oriented
introversion—extroversion
analytical—creative

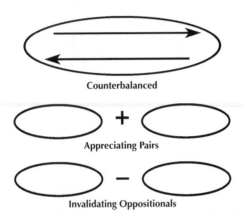

Counterbalanced

Appreciating Pairs

Invalidating Oppositionals

Hopefully, you are now developing a good understanding of the choices you have any time you encounter someone who thinks or talks in ways that upset you. You can invalidate them and waste much of your time and emotional energy trying to get them to change, or you can save energy by deciding to appreciate them and discover what is beneficial about associating with them. You can make the personal growth choice and minimize your energy investment by working to learn the benefits of thinking and feeling in paradoxical ways, if you choose.

The key question now is, how does a person who has counterbalanced, paradoxical traits know which way to respond if they don't act in socially approved, trained ways? The answer is that highly resilient people need to have things work well for themselves and others. The way they interact in any situation is guided by the feel of things, not by the form of things. In the next chapter, we'll look at how the need for good synergy is another important difference between the overly socialized, well-trained "good" child and highly resilient people. Highly resilient people act in ways helpful to others because they choose to, not because they are supposed to.

Resiliency Development Activities

1. Success is reaching a goal. Here are the steps to follow to convert the resiliency principles covered in this chapter into practice:

   ▷ Select a specific goal that you feel is moderately challenging for you, one that you probably can achieve if you apply yourself well.

   ▷ Describe the goal in a way that can be clearly measured at some point in time as having been reached or not reached.

   ▷ Spend time imagining yourself having reached the goal. Daydream about what it feels like.

   ▷ Make a list of everything that might keep you from reaching the goal. If your family might be affected, be sure to talk with them about their concerns and feelings.

   ▷ Problem solve how to avoid or handle the potential problems.

   ▷ Give yourself an extra advantage by interviewing someone who has successfully dealt with a similar challenge.

   ▷ After taking all these steps, decide whether or not you truly want to emotionally commit yourself to reaching the goal. If you make the commitment, devote yourself fully and totally to reaching the goal.

2. Carl Jung taught his patients and students how to engage in healthy self-discovery by exploring their shadow—the flaws and failings they attribute to other people. Other

psychologists have added looking at positive attributes seen in others as a reflection of one's self. Look at ways in which people that you believe exist in this world are a manifestation of your needs.

3. How do you feel about learning that your mental and emotional stability are strengthened by being complex and paradoxical? Feeling and thinking in paradoxical ways might pull you off balance if you aren't used to it, something like the first time children ride two-wheel bikes without training wheels to prop them up. Once you get the hang of it, however, a new freedom to be yourself opens up for you.

4. Engineers say that rubber-band balls, like those sold in office supply stores, bounce when dropped because they have a high "coefficient of restitution." If you appreciate ways in which physics principles can be seen to influence human behavior, use the coefficient of restitution to explain how and why people differ so widely in their ability to bounce back from extreme losses, setbacks, and disruptive change.[11]

Chapter Ten

Allowing Everything to Work Well: The Synergy Talent

While I was serving on my local school board a few years ago, a new board member was elected who kept our meetings going until late at night. Before Wally joined the board, our meetings finished at a reasonable hour, and we handled all the school district's business quite well. After Wally joined the board, he would challenge routine budget items such as purchasing a new American flag to replace an old one, and would give long lectures about not wasting taxpayer dollars. His attitude and tone were insulting at times. He assumed that all of us, board members and administrators, were irresponsible wastrels. He spoke as though he alone was dedicated to the conscientious use of taxpayer dollars.

Wally would introduce resolutions outside the scope of our board authority. He would argue at great length about administrative procedures that the board could not change because of contracts with teachers. He exceeded his authority as a board member by making demands on the district staff that had to be countermanded by the superintendent or board chairman.

Wally forced people to have to cope with him. As a state legislator from our area, he had a reputation for being contrary. Some of the points he argued made sense, but his way of raising issues had a draining effect on the board members and administrators.

School board members are elected for four-year terms. I saw grim resignation in the faces of several older members anticipating four difficult years because of Wally.

Synergistic and Desynergistic Effects

Have you ever been in a group where you had a sinking feeling when a certain person showed up? My experiences have taught me that the effect a person has on others is more important than knowing their personality tendencies.

Some people have a desynergistic effect on others. When they are present, they drain energy from a group. You feel relieved when they're absent.

Some people have synergistic effect wherever they are. When they are present, things work better for everyone. I'm sure you know several people that you enjoy serving on a committee with, having at a party, or traveling with. No matter where they are, things go better when they are present. You miss them when they are absent.

People who are highly resilient interact with others in synergistic ways. They make things work better for everyone. "Stephanie" and "Priscilla," the two organizational development specialists talked about in chapter 6, are good examples. They are people that others want to work with when success is crucial. Highly resilient people cope well with their challenges, and they usually lend a helping hand to others.

During times of crisis and change, there are always a few solid people who are generous with their concern for others. Self-confident, resilient, and compassionate, they provide reassurance and stability in chaotic situations.

A noticeable quality when you're a synergistic person is that you volunteer to help when there's trouble. You're a sort of "foul-weather friend." When things are working well, you may seem uninvolved, but when there's trouble, you show up, ready to lend a hand or take charge.

You do this, in part, to deal with your own discomfort. When other people are in pain, you feel it. When life is going well for others, you feel better. The more integrated your thoughts, feelings, and actions, the more you create a pleasant environment at home and work.

Because emotional exposure to discordant, destabilizing, and energy-draining conditions bothers you, your efforts to make things better for others is not an unselfish activity. Your synergistic nature has you acting unselfishly for selfish reasons. For your own well-being, you feel compelled to take action to improve discordant, energy-draining situations.

The term "synergy" was used first by physicians to describe how two medications taken together would lead to better results than predicted by knowing the effects of each medication taken alone. Abraham Maslow was the first psychologist to use the term "synergy" to describe differences in the effects of how managers manage their workers. While consulting with a high-tech company in California, he wrote a journal of his observations that was published later as a book titled *Eupsychian Management*. In it he described how managers in some organizations have negative impacts on the mental health of employees. Employees in these organizations leave from work psychologically depleted. They need help from their families, friends, and communities to regain enough strength to return to work. Maslow described the effect of such organizations as desynergistic; that is, the organizations drain energy out of the families and communities that their employees come from.

Maslow saw that managers in other organizations manage in ways that enhance psychological health in their employees. Away from work, their employees have happy, healthy families, contribute to community activities, and provide valuable leadership to their churches, service clubs, and other community groups. Maslow described the effect of these organizations as synergistic; that is, the organizations enhance the well-being of the families and communities their employees come from.[1]

Observe How People Affect Others

At the individual level, an ability to observe the effects that people have on others shows that identifying a person's specific personality qualities is of minor importance. For example, some introverted people are quietly and pleasantly helpful. They don't talk much, but they're always quick to offer a helping hand and seem to know just what to do that is useful. On the other hand, there are some quiet people who are always getting upset about one thing or another. They pout, withdraw, and refuse to talk about why they're upset.

Some extroverted, outgoing, talkative individuals connect well with others and get people working well together. They are the supportive glue that holds groups together. On the other hand, some extroverted talkative people always pull attention to themselves. They interrupt and intrude into what others are doing.

I'm sure you see the point. For me, whether a person is introverted or extroverted is less important than the effect a person has on others. Here are more examples.

Some people can inspire a group with their uplifting optimism, while others are oppressively optimistic. Maybe you've associated with someone who is always so smiley and cheerful, it is difficult to be around them very long.

Some people bring groups down with their depressing pessimism, while others contribute a valuable sort of practical pessimism. You'd want your attorney to anticipate everything that might go wrong and also be optimistic about resolving difficult legal matters.

Some complex, paradoxical people have no focus or direction. You would not want them in charge of anything important because they are so erratic and flaky.

I'm not saying that everyone is either synergistic or desynergistic. The majority of people are not at either extreme. Most people just drift along with whatever is happening. Things are neither better nor worse when they are present or when they are absent.

Actions Determined by Effects

When you live and function at Level Four resiliency, you are conscious of the effects of your actions on others, and you feel better when everything is working well. In other words, high-level resiliency comes from conducting yourself according to the feel of things, not by acting as you "should" or acting according to a role you have. Synergistic people are guided by what works right, not by appearances.

Good synergy is not something you make happen; it comes from losing yourself in the action of the moment. When the need for good synergy governs what you do, your personal energy blends with the energy of the people and action around you. In the workplace, this creates the harmonious kinds of optimal experiences that lead workers to report high job satisfactions.

"Achieving this unity with one's surroundings," according to psychologist Mihaly Csikszentmihalyi, "is not only an important component of enjoyable flow experiences but is also a central mechanism by which adversity is conquered." He also observed that "one of the most universal and distinctive features of the optimal experience is that people become so involved in what they are doing that the activity becomes spontaneous [and] they stop being aware of themselves as separate from the actions they are performing." High-level resiliency comes from creating positive-energy states, and then riding along when energy is flowing well—like jazz musicians do when improvising as they play.[2]

Your Intentions Pull Everything Together

Maybe you've seen a children's toy that is a human figure made up of wooden blocks held together by a string. When the string is pulled tight, the blocks all come together and the figure takes shape. When no one is pulling the string, the blocks fall limply down. The need for good synergy in your life is like the string that pulls all the parts of the toy figure together. Your healthy lifestyle, problem-solving skills, self-confidence, professionalism, paradoxical qualities, practical optimism, and efforts to become better and better are all pulled together by your synergistic need to have things work well for yourself and others.

Your way of integrating all these attributes will be unique to you and will change from situation to situation. This situational agility gives many resilient people a chameleon-like quality. They adapt the way they interact according to their sense of what is best for themselves and others in their specific situations.

· · · · · · · · · · · · · · ·

A friend of mine, Sheila, started and ran a successful insurance agency in Southern California for twenty years. Her sales records were so impressive she was often asked to speak at sales conferences. I was curious when Sheila said she did not like to make cold calls, so she never did. (In sales, a "cold call" is when a sales representative calls someone they do not know and tries to make an appointment to meet with the person to talk about that person's needs. Cold calling draws many rejections.) Sheila also said she didn't have much money in the beginning, so she decided she would find ways to make her phone ring without spending a lot of money on direct advertising.

How was Sheila successful at building a successful insurance business without either cold calling or advertising? Before she started, she spent time thinking about all the circumstances in which people buy insurance. She saw that when a home is purchased, one of the escrow requirements is that a new owner must have property-insurance coverage in place at the time of closing. Timely delivery of the insurance policy to the escrow agent is crucial. The property cannot close until the insurance is in place. No coverage, no closing.

Sheila scheduled herself to speak briefly at the morning meetings of real estate agents in her area. She arrived early with hot, fresh-baked donuts, greeted each person with friendly enthusiasm, and told the agents about the fast, reliable property insurance service she would provide for them if they sent referrals to her.

Sheila was also smart in developing friendly relationships with the secretaries and receptionists in all the real estate offices. She left her business card with them so they could contact her quickly if a sales person wanted to reach her.

Over the years, she developed a large network of Realtors, bankers, and escrow officers who funneled clients to her. After a property closed, she would arrange to meet the new owners to congratulate them and give them a gift. She worked at developing a personal relationship with them, then followed up by offering to take care of their auto-insurance and life-insurance needs.

As Sheila's business grew, she acquired more and more Hispanic home buyers as customers. She learned conversational Spanish and became fluent in it. Through her efforts over the years, Sheila built a profitable agency that had over 3,000 accounts—without ever making cold calls.

Start with Questions, Focus on Results

To access and develop your synergistic skills, do the following:

▶ Approach new, unstable, or difficult situations with this question in mind: "How can I interact with this so that things turn out well for everyone?"

▶ Look for creative ways to help make things work well. Ask others, "What would you like to have happen?" Volunteer in a way that lets others refuse your help if they wish.

▶ Recognize that you have selfish reasons for wanting to have things work well for others, and admit this to yourself.

▶ Tell yourself it's all right to be successful at what you do and be paid well, without working too hard! Synergistic people focus on energy management, not time management.

▶ Learn the difference between allowing things to work well and making things work well.

▶ Pause occasionally and quiet your mind. Scan all around you to see if your intuition is picking up anything. It is comforting to know you can count on subliminal perception—a sort of internal sonar—to signal an alert to danger, locate useful information, or deliver creative solutions.

> ► At the end of each day, review the effects of your actions. Did your day flow smoothly? Was a meeting productive because of you? Did you help someone handle something better?

A sign that you have developed a synergistic nature is that you accomplish more with less effort. Your life flows along pleasantly and smoothly. People who are synergistic think not of time management but of energy management. You get all the important things done and still have spare time to do what you enjoy.

Become the "Go-To" Person

In every organization, there are a few individuals that people go to when something really important must be handled right. People who need to have things work well are the ones called on to deal with uniquely difficult and challenging situations. Here's an example. Bob Foley was a senior hospital administrator who had a reputation for being skillful at handling difficult projects. Bob says:

"I was told by the administrator of the large hospital where I worked that I had to manage the employee and visitor parking requirements during a major construction project. I did not want this assignment because the last time this had been done, it was a mess. It cost the hospital a lot of money, and almost everyone was unhappy. I discussed my concern with the administrator, but he gave me no choice. He said to run the project in the same manner as was done before and just put up with the complaints.

"That attitude wasn't in accordance with how I do things, so I decided to learn everything I could about why the failures occurred during the last project and then design solutions to solve the problems. When I talked with employees, I heard that one of the problems before was that the temporary parking lots were located several miles away and that shuttle buses ran only every thirty minutes. So if an employee got off work and missed the shuttle by three minutes, he or she had to stand and wait almost half an hour until the next bus came.

As a consequence, many employees got home late for family activities. Some employees told me they would demand overtime pay for this time.

"My solution was to run buses every fifteen minutes and have the drivers be more responsive. but I still had complaints. I knew there had to be a better way.

"As I was coming to work one morning I noticed that churches near the hospital all had empty parking lots. I immediately went to all the nearby churches and offered to upgrade their parking lots with lights and repaving in exchange for free parking for a year. The churches would still have their parking lots for services on Saturdays, Sundays, and certain evenings, but these lots could give us many weekday and nighttime parking spaces within walking distance of the hospital. Every church except one agreed. Once this was in place, everyone could park close enough to walk to and from the hospital. Except for still needing one remote lot for Sunday mornings, this eliminated the need for most buses and drivers.

"The new construction took longer than expected—almost a year and a half, but the churches let me negotiate an extension, so everything worked out well. The result was far better than the previous experience. We had far fewer employee and visitor complaints, and the hospital saved almost one million dollars from the original projected costs."

Since then, Foley has taken a position as vice president with a large corporation where he continues to use creative methods for making things run smoother and better at a lower cost. His success is not from applying what he learned in management school, but from knowing that, somehow, in some way, things can work better. There are no books or seminars, for example, on how to manage employee parking during the construction of a new hospital wing. It takes a synergistic person to handle a uniquely difficult challenge like that. It takes someone like Bob Foley to be guided by an inner compass—someone who asks questions, scans the total situation with empathy, and invents creative solutions that work well for everyone.

Foley says he also makes himself useful "by becoming an expert on a subject that others have no interest in. Also, and more importantly, the task then becomes fun. It becomes a game that allows creativity to be applied to the task."[3]

But There Can Be a Downside...

Being synergistic is not without challenges! A reality of life is that every way of existing on this planet has problems. If you're synergistic, people know that things run much better when you're involved. As a result, you can receive too many requests to chair committees, take on more responsibilities at work, and assume more leadership roles in groups, more than you can possibly handle. To protect your limited time and energy, sustain your health, and have time for your family, you may find yourself having to say no to many requests—sometimes to groups or causes that are important to you.

Sometimes synergistic people run into problems by making things work too well. A former college classmate took me to lunch one day and told me about a problem she had at work because she was too effective! She was a department manager in a large state agency. She had trained her staff so well and organized her department so efficiently that when upper-level administrators came into her area, some of them were bothered to see public employees relaxed, calm, and friendly. In most other departments, the atmosphere was hectic, the workers look tired and drained. A senior administrator had told her more than once that some executives had complained to him that her department must not have enough work to do.

She had documented for her boss that her department was producing more work per person, of higher quality, with fewer errors, at a faster rate than any comparable department. But the upper-level grumbling continued. Her people did not appear to be working hard enough as state employees.

She eventually became fed up with receiving criticism instead of praise for her outstanding managing skills. She resigned, took her retirement money, and opened a pasta shop in a mall. More fun for her, but a great loss to the state.

Empathy Is Essential

Once in awhile, I will meet with people professionally to help them problem solve a difficult situation. Before I agree, however, I ask them to tell me how others in the situation might describe what is happening. I listen to see if the person seems to have an accurate understanding of how things appear from the perspectives of others. If the person lacks empathy skills, I won't agree to work with them. People who lack empathy do not have a good understanding of how they may be contributing to their problems with others. People who have a desynergistic, energy-draining effect on groups and families have little empathy for people bothered by their actions.

The ability to have things working well for yourself and others requires empathy—an accurate understanding of what other people are thinking and feeling. When you live and work in a synergistic way, you are attuned to what is going on with others. Empathic awareness of another person comes from asking such questions as

+ How is that person experiencing what is happening?
+ How does that person feel?
+ What does she see?
+ What might he do?

These sorts of questions open your mind to understand another person's needs, his or her feelings, viewpoints, and so on. When you look at what is happening from the viewpoint of others, you increase your chances of finding a creative solution to a problem.

Here's an example. Budget cuts in a state agency led to the elimination of an environmental regulatory department. The scientists working in the department were dismayed. They'd been conducting federally mandated testing; the state had to do the testing to receive federal funding and avoid sanctions. When the scientists looked at the situation from the perspective of state administrators, they saw that the work would have to be contracted out. Knowing they were the best qualified people in the region to do the work, they formed a consulting firm, bid for the job, and won the contract. They

liked the outcome, because as consultants they paid themselves more than they had earned as state employees.

As with other resiliency qualities, there can be a down-
side to empathy. The same sensitivity that leads to having
things working well also exposes you to distress in others.
Empathy for other people's feelings requires a counterbalancing quality of toughness to not be controlled by their pain.
This is why I have suggested to a few people that they would
benefit from a workshop on "insensitivity training."

Difficult People Are No Longer Difficult for You

Rough times can be even more difficult when you must deal
with people who act in ways that can be energy draining.
Someone has an energy-draining effect on others, however,
only with people who lack skills for handling what he or she
says or does. As discussed in chapter 4, a major benefit gained
from learning how to handle your emotions well is that you
can maintain your emotional stability when interacting with
emotionally upset people.

High-level resiliency includes being able to gain control
quickly with an angry person, divert personal attacks, remain
immune to negative talk, and cope well with dysfunctional people. This level of ability includes accepting and believing the
following guidelines:

+ Every person gets to think and talk the way they do.

+ If others talk and think in ways that bother you, there is
  nothing wrong with them; it is you who has the problem
  of not being able to handle hearing such talk.

+ People who talk in ways that you find difficult to handle
  can be converted into teachers in disguise. Ask yourself
  what your blind spots are and what you can learn when
  you experience someone as difficult.

You will not be effective with anyone that you invalidate
as a human being. If any part of your self-concept is based on
using a demeaned anti-model to serve as a contrast for your
identity needs, you need such people in your world; you will

never be able to change them or rid yourself of their presence in your life. When you have strong, conscious self-esteem and a healthy self-concept, you do not need anti-models to build yourself up.

Your ability to create optimal conditions is strengthened the more that you can exercise compassionate empathy for people who act and talk in ways that drain your energy, if you let it happen. Use questions to look past their behavior to find how to neutralize or assimilate what they do.

Let's go back to Wally, the school board member. While Wally was making a speech to our almost empty boardroom late one night, I decided to stop being irritated with him and find a way to handle him better. I asked myself, "Why is he doing this?" Once I asked the question, the answer came to me. Wally was a politician and did not have an outside source of income other than his pay as a state legislator. Our board meetings were tape recorded and transcribed. He used the situation to obtain free written transcripts of his political positions. In most cases, his motions were so far removed from board business, no one would second them. On this particular night, he wanted the school board to pass a resolution declaring that no businesses in our county should engage in trade with South Africa.

I knew that trying to get Wally to stop being so contrary and disruptive was a negative goal. Trying to get someone to stop doing something that you don't like is an almost impossible goal to achieve. On the positive side, I appreciated that he was stirring up some interesting debates of a kind that we had not had before he joined the board.

I thought up a positive plan of action. At the end of the next board meeting, immediately after we adjourned, I walked over to him and said, "Wally, I want to thank you for bringing up controversial subjects the way you do. It's good for us, and I hope you keep it up."

Wally said, "Huh?" He stared at me and mumbled, "Thank you." But he was startled and puzzled. He was accustomed to people telling him to shut up. Being thanked and encouraged was not something he was used to.

It's amazing what happens when you ask people to do what they're going to do anyway. If one of their purposes is to prove that no one can control them, your request throws them off balance, and you are now in control.

What I did with Wally was like an emotional, martial arts move. I pulled him in the opposite way from what he was expecting. This threw his energy off balance. I followed up in future meetings by empathizing with his views. When he took a position against a motion, I would inquire to see if I understood him and would then suggest another argument in favor of his position. He was surprised and puzzled when I did this, and it did not bother him that when the vote was held, the tally was usually six to one against him.

One month when we had some difficult school district boundary decisions to make, I telephoned him the night before. I said, "Wally, the board has some complex issues to resolve tomorrow night. Can I count on you to be there and let me know if the board is overlooking something important?"

He said, "Al, I'll be there."

In the months that followed, Wally became less and less confrontational. Our meetings began adjourning at a decent time again, and he and I became friendly. To my great surprise, after almost three years on our school board, Wally resigned. In his letter of resignation, he said our school district was so well run, it did not need his attention.

I'm not saying that my way of interacting with Wally will get you the same results with someone you experience as difficult. No one method or strategy is guaranteed. Remember, a can opener can't open a can unless you use it correctly. The technique itself isn't what changed things with Wally; it was how I used it that led to things working better for us all.

Instead of passing judgment on difficult people, empathize with them. This changes the energy. With empathy, you can neutralize their desynergistic actions and create better synergy.

Empathy is not the same as sympathy. *Sympathy* is to experience the same feelings that another person is feeling. Close friends feel each other's pains and joys as their own.

Empathy is to accurately comprehend what others are

feeling while maintaining your own separate emotional state. The best caregivers have excellent empathy skills, but must avoid sympathy or else they develop "bystander" post traumatic stress disorder and experience emotional burnout.

Empathy is easiest with people you care for and who like you. In my workshops I use the term "compathy" to describe times when it takes emotional strength and emotional intelligence to listen with compassionate understanding to people who are angry or upset with you.

Here are some well-tested compathy steps for resolving conflicts with angry people:[4]

- ▶ Ask them to tell you what's upsetting them.
- ▶ Listen carefully.
- ▶ Ask one or two clarifying questions.
- ▶ Repeat back what you heard them say.
- ▶ Validate their feelings. Express understanding for what they feel.
- ▶ Thank them for telling you to your face what has upset them. It is better that they talk directly to you than behind your back to others.
- ▶ Add a point that supports their case.
- ▶ Ask what their request is; what do they want?
- ▶ Once they start talking about what they want or request, discuss possible solutions with them.

When angry people feel well heard, they usually calm down. In fact, many people will apologize later for being angry. Highly resilient, synergistic people have strong empathy skills. They have the ability to see things from another person's point of view—even someone they dislike. Compathy is a valuable high-level skill.

The primary goal of empathy in a challenging situation is to fully comprehend the thinking and needs of others so you can develop an effective plan of action. Understanding how things look to someone who is threatening the success of your efforts may seem like a peculiar skill to develop, but asking yourself how the other person views things may be the key that dissolves the conflict. Compathy for others will make you more aware of what you can do or say in times of turmoil to stabilize what is happening.

Develop Deep Resiliency by Developing Your Synergy Skills

What do resilient people do when they aren't having to be resilient? They're creating optimal conditions for themselves and others.

Why is developing synergistic skills important? When you know what conditions of good synergy are like, and know it is possible to create them, you have an inner understanding of what you are bouncing back to.

The more you develop your synergy skills, the more you develop your ability to be resilient during rough times. Signs that your way of interacting is synergistic include the following items:

✦ With you around, meetings run more smoothly, people work together better, equipment runs efficiently, and the atmosphere at work is more pleasant.

✦ At work you may seem to have an easy job. That's true. Your job is easier because you worked hard to make it that way.

✦ You remain relaxed and enjoy times when there is an easy flow to everything. You can sit back and let things run themselves when everything is working well. You expend less energy than others doing routine work, but you can put strong, sustained energy into essential tasks.

✦ You notice and take care of the little things that make a difference in how well things work. You detect early indications of potential trouble and take action to prevent them, while feeling little concern about matters that you know will not be problems.

✦ You have a high tolerance for uncertainty and ambiguity.

You do not need definite answers and certainty about unfolding events as much as others, and may hold back from jumping to conclusions that others assume are right. At the same time, your feeling for energy patterns allows you to quickly draw meaningful conclusions from small amounts of information before others can see what is happening.

+ You feel comfortable at the control point between counterbalanced, oppositional tension within groups. You encourage people to express opposing views and opinions. You can understand each side's position and help them work out a resolution. You are a good arbitrator and facilitator when strong conflicts develop.

+ You act in ethical ways that increase the respect and trust you receive from others.

+ You enjoy and feel delighted with the accomplishments of others. You let others know how much you appreciate them.

+ You feel happy. You enjoy your life and your work. You have a playful spirit that lets you laugh and frequently be amused. People like your sense of humor.

+ You trust your intuition.[5] When you sense that something is wrong, you investigate. When you sense that everything is fine, you don't let yourself be misled by the fears or worries of others.[6]

+ You work on future events so that when they occur things fall into place easily without last-minute scrambling.

+ You have optional time for being curious about new developments.

+ You respond to an emergency or crisis with calm optimism; you expect everything to turn out well.

An additional benefit from living and working in these ways is that you strengthen your resiliency at all levels. By remaining calm and relaxed during periods of intense of action, your health and well-being become even more optimal. Your awareness of many details and understanding of how things work improves your problem-solving skills. Your daily successes strengthen your three inner selfs.

As you master all four levels of resiliency, you become better and better at handling high levels of change and can thrive in rough situations that overwhelm others. And beyond that, because of your synergistic nature, you have energy for helping other people get through rough times as well.

The next chapter shows what is possible at Level Five resiliency. It describes how at the highest level of resiliency development, you are able to convert misfortune into good fortune, and convert setbacks into unique opportunities.

Resiliency Development Activities

1. Reflect on what you've learned here. Take a few moments to describe people you know who are very good to have involved in important projects. What is it that they do that makes them valuable?

2. How good are your empathy skills? Practice understanding and explaining in the best possible light why others act, think, and feel as they do.

3. Review the steps for handling an angry person with compathy skills. Plan ahead to the next time you encounter an angry person. Afterward evaluate yourself on how well you did.

4. Do you trust your intuition? Have you ever had a hunch or feeling, talked yourself out of it, and later regretted that you did? Did you learn a useful lesson?

5. At the end of chapter 1, you were challenged to identify an unstated, essential aspect of resiliency. What do you think it is?[7]

Chapter Eleven

Strengthening Your Talent for Serendipity

Stories told to us in childhood can have lasting effects on us. When Horace Walpole was a child, his mother read him ancient Persian fairy tales such as Scheherazade's stories about Ali Baba, Sinbad the sailor, and Aladdin. As an adult he recalled that he enjoyed hearing "a silly fairy tale called 'The Three Princes of Serendip.' As their highnesses traveled, they were always making discoveries, by accidents and sagacity, of things which they were not in quest of...." In a letter he wrote to a friend on January 28, 1754, Walpole said he had created the word "serendipity" to describe a talent he had—an ability to discover good fortune in accidents and misfortune.

Serendipity, according to Walpole, comes from using wisdom to convert an unexpected event, accident, or mishap into good fortune. He said that three elements must be present for serendipity to occur.

First, something unexpected or accidental happens to you. Second, your perceptiveness, good sense, and wisdom (sagacity), lead you to discover the third element—an unexpected benefit, gift, or blessing in what happened.

In the Persian fairy tale that delighted Walpole, the three princes of Serendip used their powers of observation and their problem-solving skills to make an endless series of difficult circumstances turn out well. Walpole was fascinated with the notion that we humans have the ability to discover accidental good fortune, and he learned how to do this himself.[1]

Serendipity: Converting a Life-Disrupting Event into Good Luck

Serendipity is an advanced-level resiliency skill. Individuals with many basic resiliency strengths are often able to convert a life-disrupting experience into one of the best things that ever happened. This is more than bouncing back; while struggling to cope with a life-disrupting event, you find new strengths and may discover unexpected opportunities. You see that you can take your life or your career in a new direction that would not have opened up to you without the disruptive event. The adversity creates an opportunity for taking your life in a different and better direction than you expected.

* * * * * * * * * * * * * *

Jesse Reeder graduated from college with a master's degree and began working for a mid-sized electric utility. Her technical background, skills with people, and constant motivation to learn led to a series of promotions. Five years later, the five-member board of directors selected her to be the general manager and chief executive officer of the utility. Still in her forties, Jesse was the only woman CEO of an electric utility of its size in the United States. When I interviewed Jesse, she told me, "I loved my job, I was dedicated, and I worked long hours. I couldn't imagine doing anything else."

Jesse was an excellent CEO. She heard no significant complaints from anyone about service, operations, or financial matters. But at a monthly board of directors meeting, three newly elected board members held a surprise vote and fired her. They gave her until eight o'clock the next morning to clear out her office.

"Everything happened so fast," Jesse says, "it seemed unreal." When reporters swarmed around her after the vote, she says she vividly remembers "separating from my body into a peaceful observer's role." The reporters were expecting her to be distraught or angry. But instead, Jesse remained calm and answered their questions with self-confidence.

The impact of the evening's events triggered Jesse into an altered state of high consciousness. She recalls feeling fascinated with being a highly aware, calm, observer of the action, noticing and understanding everything that was happening around her.

She expressed her concern that the board's decision had not been fully considered. She reassured the reporters that the utility employees were skilled and would continue to provide excellent service.

In the weeks that followed, intense public scrutiny of her record showed that her management of the utility had been outstanding. Four months later, under threat of being recalled in a special election, the three board members who fired her resigned from the board. When new board members were appointed to fill the three empty positions, the new board of directors extended the application period for the CEO position. They contacted Jesse, asked her to please apply for her old job, and offered to raise her salary.

Jesse felt torn. She says she loved being CEO of the utility, but the impact of the way she was fired opened her to new ways of thinking and being. Her memory of how she reacted to the crisis awakened within her a way of being present with events that she hadn't known was possible. She declined the opportunity to be reinstated as the CEO. She chose, instead, to go on an inner journey to discover what had happened and allow herself to be changed by the process.

She says, "Being fired the way I was, was an epiphany. I learned that I was a survivor. Before that I had been terrified of being fired. That experience made me realize that if I could live through that and handle it, then I can handle anything."

Highly resilient people have a knack for finding a hidden gift in adversity. Jesse's self-esteem and her self-concept were not tied to having the job title of CEO. Strong self-confidence allowed Jesse to go through a ten-year process of inner exploration and work as a consultant to develop ways of teaching others how to skillfully handle difficult challenges and to avoid getting stuck in negative states. She founded a company that offers "Self-Mastery" workshops and wrote *Black Holes and Energy Pirates,* a creative perspective on the ways that people affect each other's energies.

Jesse is very happy with her new life. She says it took a

long time to get over being fired, but emphasizes, "It was the best thing that could have happened to me."[2]

Questions Can Lead to Discovering a Gift

Jesse converted the experience of being fired into a life-transforming event. The art of resiliency usually starts with looking for the hidden benefits in difficulties by asking questions like those that Bill Harris listed (chapter 3):

+ What's good about this?
+ How can I turn this to my advantage?
+ What unusual opportunity has this created?

Questions can prepare your mind to discover benefits in events that would upset other people. Here's a minor example from my own experience. After I was discharged from the paratroopers, I needed a summer job before returning to college. I looked around and decided to take a position as park director in a large city park. It had softball and football fields, tennis courts, and playgrounds for children. There were many areas with picnic tables and benches under tall fir trees. The play area for younger children had teeter-totters and a shallow, circular wading pool.

I enjoyed playing games and doing crafts with the children who came to the park each day. One of the hassles I had as park director was to prevent a group of older boys from riding their bikes into the children's wading pool and racing around the edge. They would do this sometimes even when there were little kids in the pool, which worried and upset the children's parents. I asked the boys to stop, and some did, but several of them would still swoop into the park on their bikes, race around the inside of the pool three or four times, and then race out of the park before I could catch them.

One day, as I stood watching the boys race way on their bikes, I thought to myself, "There's got to be a practical way to stop them from doing this. What can I do?"

When I went to work the next Monday morning, I discovered that during the weekend five park benches had been thrown into the children's wading pool. I was about to take off my shoes to wade in and pull the benches out when I stopped. I thought to myself, "Wait a minute! This is a solution to the problem with the boys who ride their bikes in the pool!" I saw that the benches in the pool would block the bike riders. I pulled out several benches, but left three in the pool in places that would prevent any bikes from circling around. During the day, I was delighted seeing that the little children loved having the benches to climb and play on. My supervisor wasn't very happy when she came by later in the week saw the benches in the pool, but I managed to convince her that they eliminated a dangerous risk.

An amazing thing about your brain is that when you instruct it to look for something, it often finds it. We humans can have two different sets of feelings about our experiences. It's not a matter of feeling one way or the other, as in feeling happy or unhappy. If you define a situation too narrowly and think of it only as ruining your life, then information that seems contrary to your mind set, such as possible good fortune or opportunity, can't reach you. People who turn intrusive or unwanted events into accidental opportunities do so because they deliberately scan for those opportunities.

"I should have listened to my wife!"

Tom Peterson worked for many years to build a strong business selling television sets, stereo systems, and home appliances. He gave people good value, a full-satisfaction guarantee, and friendly service. With the help of his wife Gloria, who handled the books, Tom developed an excellent reputation. He was proud of his high percentage of repeat customers.

Tom advertised heavily on television and in newspapers. He became known for his trademark crew cut and his cheery early-morning television commercials.

In 1990, Tom was approached by the owners of a competing company, Stereo Super Stores. They wanted him to buy them out. The price was very attractive. He examined their books, looked at their inventory, talked to employees, sized up the store locations, and looked at the leases. Everything looked good. Here was a chance to eliminate a competitor and more than double his business. His bankers said they would loan him whatever he needed to make the purchase.

Before making his final decision, Tom asked Gloria what she thought about the acquisition. She told him that the numbers looked good, but something didn't feel right to her. He asked her to explain why, but she couldn't. She told him she had a strong feeling that he shouldn't acquire Stereo Super Stores.

Tom was so self-confident, however, and so convinced that this was a rare opportunity that should not be passed up, he went ahead and made the purchase. Within months, he discovered that he had made a serious mistake. He found he had paid far too much for a dying company. He worked harder than ever to save his business, but he couldn't turn things around. Three years later, he was close to bankruptcy. He was about to lose everything, including his original business.

Tom was one of the most well-known businessmen in his region. When highly visible people make mistakes, their mistakes are highly visible. The major newspaper in his region ran a feature story about him and his mistake. Tom felt embarrassed, but he is a resilient survivor. He looked at his situation. He and Gloria asked each other what they could do to survive and turn the situation around.

Tom decided to openly admit his mistake and, instead of getting bogged down in foreclosure lawsuits, focus his energies on saving and rebuilding his original business. He also saw that he had made a big mistake by not listening to his wife and that he needed to learn from the experience. During the week after the newspaper story, he made a new television commercial that started with him saying:

"This is Tom Peterson, and I confess I should have listened to my wife! When Gloria told me not to buy Stereo Super Stores, I should have listened to her. I made a mistake, but we're still in business—with a new name. We are now 'Tom Peterson and Gloria's Too.' We have some great bargains for you at the old store this weekend...."

Tom played up his mistake in judgment. He dealt with the crisis in a way that endeared him to many people and increased their respect for him. Old customers flocked into his original main store. To survive financially, Tom had to close all the Stereo Super Store outlets, close a warehouse, lay off many employees, and shift product lines. He began to use a supply system management method he had never attempted before. He advertised products in newspaper and television ads while freight trucks from the manufacturers were en route to his store.

He explains, "At first it didn't feel right to advertise products that weren't sitting in a warehouse. It took courage to trust that the freight trucks would be docking at the back of the store a few hours before customers walked in the front." Tom grins and says, "In the years before my struggle to survive, I was turning inventory three times a year. Now I'm turning inventory twelve times a year with fewer employees and higher profit margins! I'm thankful that I almost lost the business. Gloria and I are much better off financially than before."[3]

Some Life-Transforming Events Come from Inside

Thousands of people are diagnosed with cancer each year. Many people react as though the diagnostic finding is a death sentence. Some people turn the illness into a life-transforming experience. Lynne Massie is one of those. Lynne felt waves of anxiety and panic when she was told that the tumor in her breast was too large to be removed by lumpectomy; that she must have a mastectomy, followed by chemotherapy and radiation treatment.

Lynne started asking many questions about the doctors, the treatments, and her future. "Reading book after book about survivors," she says, "one thing becomes evident. Almost without fail, those cancer victims who survive terrible odds take charge of their lives spiritually and holistically."

During what felt like an exhausting marathon of treatments, Lynne examined her life and what was important to her. She wrote poems about her feelings and shared them with her family, friends, and minister. She decided that one way to beat cancer was to fill her days with enjoyable activities such as playing golf and showing her beloved purebred dogs at dog shows.

Now cancer free for many years, Lynne says that "cancer became not the enemy, but the teacher. Length of life is inconsequential. It is truly the quality of the journey. Living each day in alignment with my internal truth, in a matter that is totally congruent inside and out, is beating cancer to the ultimate."[4]

* * * * * * * * * * * * * *

When Marcia Keith became president of her university association, the first column she wrote for the association newsletter was titled "The Benefits of Breast Cancer." Marcia revealed that she had had two cancer surgeries when she was thirty. "Eight years after my first operation, I developed cancer in both breasts, so I had a double mastectomy, followed by a year of radiation and chemotherapy. I am now a twenty-five-year cancer survivor and have lived the last eighteen years cancer-free.

"I've always believed that the cancer would not kill me, that I will die from something else. I'm glad I had cancer. The benefits have been great. I'm now a stronger person and I'm very active doing today what I realize I might not be able to do tomorrow.

"I stay in good health by following a sensible diet and exercising on a regular basis. I enjoy walking, golf, and yoga. And, a big stretch for me, I've also learned to allow myself to be cared for by others. Some of my strength came from a group of friends who have been together for thirty years and are known affectionately as 'The Ladies.' They have saved me thousands of dollars in psychotherapy!

"I'm now cancer-free, but not free of cancer's effects. I now know in a way that I never truly knew before that I will die—and I know that I may die as soon as today or tomorrow. That knowledge changes things. It makes my friends more dear. It makes my family more valuable. It makes most problems unworthy of anguish. It makes having fun very important. It makes having love in my life the most crucial goal. It makes today a gift and tomorrow a dream. Having had breast cancer has made my life fuller and richer. These are the benefits I have derived from having breast cancer."[5]

* * * * * * * * * * * * * *

Among the people you know, there are some like Lynne Massie and Marcia Keith who have been transformed by going through difficult, defining times and have emerged thankful for what they went through. If you ask around and take time to listen, you will hear some amazing, inspiring stories.

Being Fired Can Lead to a Profound Transformation

A deep test of resiliency is having to recover from having your life ripped apart both externally and internally. Paul Wieand was a smart, highly motivated, exceptionally successful young banker. At age thirty-one, he became president of Independence Bancorp, a bank with over with over 1,000 employees and $2 billion in deposits. Not content to remain president, Paul worked aggressively to rise higher. By the time he was thirty-seven, he was certain that at the next board meeting he would be elected to replace the retiring chief executive officer. He had lobbied and cultivated the bank's board members and alerted them to flaws in his main competitor for the CEO position.

To celebrate his expected promotion, Paul took his wife to Paris for two weeks. He enjoyed his first-class vacation and living like an important executive.

His first morning back at the bank, Paul was surprised to find the outgoing CEO and the bank's attorney waiting for him in his office. They handed him a letter of resignation, saying that if he signed it, they would arrange a generous "golden parachute" separation package for him.

Paul felt waves of panic. "Why? What?" he stammered. They explained that his competitor for the CEO position was well-liked and well-respected by most of the board members. Paul's back-stabbing way of trying to eliminate his competition had backfired. The board decided they didn't want a CEO who used his sort of tactics, even though they respected his bank-managing skills.

Paul was experienced at making important decisions quickly. He saw the advantages of not fighting and doing as they wished. He signed the letter and left the building.

He felt emotionally shattered. In the weeks that followed, he drifted into a deep depression. He lost fifteen pounds. He felt he lost everything even though by most standards he was wealthy. "Without my position at the bank," he says, "I didn't know who I was. I lost my identity."

As weeks and months passed, Paul asked himself, "Who am I?" and "Why am I here?" He began to see that his identity—who he was—had come from acting out a role in a corporation. Without his job title and status, he felt like nothing.

He realized he had to find his inner identity. His solution was to create a new professional life for himself by going to graduate school. He enrolled in a doctoral program in psychology and began working to earn a PhD.

Paul's doctoral program included working in a state hospital with psychiatric patients. At the hospital, he became interested in patients with IQs over 150 who were diagnosed as schizophrenic. He started a therapy group with them. While working with this group, Paul found that revealing his private secrets and answering their questions with total honesty led them to reveal their secrets and feelings to him and to each other. His honesty created an atmosphere of trust and authenticity that led to impressive progress with the patients in the group.

Paul began to wonder, "If an atmosphere of trust and authenticity works with people isolated from others by their schizophrenia, shouldn't it also work with corporate leaders I know who are isolated from others by their roles?" He decided to find out.

In 1995, Paul Wieand opened the Center for Advanced Emotional Intelligence at his estate in Pennsylvania. He began offering a unique program for executives. He and his partner, Jan Birchfield, have helped dozens of executives learn how to be authentic in their communications, reveal feelings honestly, understand how their strengths can be weaknesses, develop strong inner identities, and become clear in their values. Graduates of his program report breakthroughs they had never imagined possible.[6]

Serendipity Is Not Synchronicity or Good Luck

Many people confuse serendipity with good luck and synchronicity. Serendipity is not a lucky accident. An example of accidental luck would be to purchase a deteriorated old house, and when you begin to restore it, you discover an old painting hidden up in the attic that is worth more than what you paid for the house.

Synchronicity is when *external* forces impact us in meaningful ways that are far beyond rational comprehension. Synchronicity refers to extraordinary, meaningful coincidences where one feels that something more than chance is involved. Research by quantum physicists is opening many people to understand that we are all immersed in a connected sea of energies in which all things have a sympathetic connection. When you are emotionally attuned to such reality, you may notice coincidences that other people miss or dismiss.

• • • • • • • • • • • • • • •

When synchronicity occurs, it may feel like a cosmic joke or as if some powerful force is toying with you. Hiro Hayashida, a colleague of mine in Japan, says, "When I moved to Tokyo, I looked for an apartment to rent. I checked several locations, but none of them appealed to me. At one apartment, however, I knew at my first glance it was the right place for me and rented it immediately. I moved in the next morning.

"That afternoon, the postal service delivered a personal letter to my apartment addressed to 'Mr. Hayashida.' I was puzzled about how a letter could be written to me and delivered to me at my new address the day I moved in. I opened the letter and discovered it had not been written to me, but to the former tenant of that room. I got a chill! The apartment I'd felt was exactly right for me had been recently occupied by a man with the same name.

"I felt the hair stand up on my back and neck, because my name is very rare. Unlike in China, Japan has thousands of surnames. In my forty-two years of life, I've known of only four persons who have the same name as mine (apart from my relatives). I decided then that I would see more than just coincidence in this happening. I decided to see that always there is more going on in this world than I may understand, and I believe these synchronicities will eventually turn out to my favor."

An Art Is Something You Must Work to Develop

Serendipity is an art to be mastered. Serendipity is when you purposefully use your *internal* mental and emotional abilities to convert what could be a loss or setback into a positive or beneficial incident.

The art of serendipity is a powerful, self-created antidote to grief, despair, and feeling like a victim. This ability explains how some people not only recover, they transform themselves into a better way of being because of the bad experiences they've gone through. The starting place for converting misfortune into good fortune often starts by asking questions such as, "What is good about what happened?" Here is where the creative problem-solving abilities developed at Level Two resiliency blossom as a high-level life skill.

When you become highly resilient, you have an advantage. You can turn a disruptive event or adversity into a desirable development. When you're hit by an unexpected crisis, you don't let yourself feel victimized; you go from being upset to coping, to thriving, to serendipity with amazing speed.

From now on, when you think about a difficult past experience or tell others about one of your roughest challenges, include why it was good for you. By applying what you've learned in your resiliency program, you can, like Jesse Reeder, Tom Peterson, Lynne Massie, Marcia Keith, and Paul Wieand, find meaning and positive value in difficult experiences. You can neutralize painful memories with the benefits you gain. This ability brings you depth of understanding, inner peace, and wisdom.

The new knowledge about resiliency psychology shows that people can learn how to turn misfortune into good fortune and gain strength from life's worst trials. Your efforts to bounce back from a life-disrupting experience can lead to the emergence of strengths you did not know you had, and can be turned into one of the best things that ever happened to you.

The next chapter describes how some amazingly resilient people are able to convert extreme misfortune into good luck and respond to shattering experiences by allowing themselves to be transformed into a better way of being.

Resiliency Development Activities

1. Recall a difficult experience in your past, looking for value found in what you went through. When you search for meaning and something positive, ask yourself these questions:

   ▷ What can I learn from the experience that is useful?

   ▷ Why might I be thankful that I had that experience? How was it good for me?

   ▷ What new strengths did I gain? In what ways did I develop self-confidence? In what ways have I become more understanding?

2. Here is a summary of effective resiliency responses, attitudes, and abilities that strengthen your talent for serendipity:

   ▷ Calm yourself. When caught off guard by bad news or misfortune, you can tap into your resiliency strengths by telling yourself to relax, taking a deep breath, and talking to yourself. Some repeat a saying such as, "In stormy times, I look for a rainbow."

   ▷ Orient quickly. Ask resiliency questions. What is my new reality? What would be useful for me to do right now?

   ▷ Commit yourself totally to surviving and coping. Misfortune can bring out your deeper strengths when you repeat to yourself, "Somehow, in some way, I'm going to handle this and make things turn out well."

   ▷ Problem solve by being curious and playful. Toy with the crisis. Poke fun at it. Experiment with your perspective. Scan others with empathy. Ask, "What are other people thinking and feeling about what's happening?"

▷ Laugh. Laughter relaxes you. If you can't laugh, cry. One way or another, release tensions and calm yourself. Do whatever you must to regain emotional balance.

▷ Choose to accept what's happening. Highly resilient survivors do not waste energy protesting against what has happened. They react to a crisis or disruptive life event as though they wanted it to happen. Their attitude is, "Everything happens the way it should."

▷ Ask serendipity questions. Why is it good that this happened? Is there an opportunity here that did not exist before? What could I do to turn this around and have it turn out well for all of us?

▷ Take action. Do something different. Be creative or impulsive. Do anything that might in some way lead to a good outcome. Remember: When what you're doing isn't working, do something else!

3. Validate and anchor serendipity thinking by talking with someone who has been though a life-transforming experience. He or she may be a cancer survivor, a survivor of a personal tragedy, or a survivor of devastating financial losses or a career setback. Interview the person to find out how they coped and why they see value in what they went through.

Chapter Twelve

Mastering Extreme Resiliency Challenges

Survivors of extreme trauma are never the same again. Their lives have two parts: "before" and "after." How their new life turns out for them depends on their resiliency.

●　●　●　●　●　●　●　●　●　●　●　●　●　●

Skip Wilkins was a star athlete in high school. He set records in track and football and won many awards. During his senior year, he received letters from over twenty college coaches trying to recruit him.

Three days after Skip graduated from high school, he broke his neck while water skiing. As he lay in the water near the shore, he was conscious, but he couldn't feel anything or move his body. He'd been injured before, but this was different. He felt panicky and bewildered as paramedics picked him up, strapped him onto a stretcher, placed him in an ambulance, and sped to the hospital with sirens blaring.

Skip's father, Tom Wilkins, clenched his teeth when saw his son on the examining table in the emergency room. Tom was an ex-paratrooper who had been an outstanding athlete himself in boxing, football, tumbling, and swimming. He'd seen many athletic injuries. He knew immediately that his son's injury was very bad. He realized his son's future would be life in a wheelchair. He reached down and clasped his son's lifeless hand. He bent over and looked into his son's terrified eyes. "Skip... Son...," he said, trying not to choke up. "You've got... you've got a broken neck."

The neurosurgeon shaved Skip's head, then drilled screws into his skull to anchor the device that would immobilize his head and neck. The weeks that followed were agony for Skip. Every day and night someone would be at his bedside doing some procedure to his helpless body.

The break in his neck was low enough that he could breath on his own and turn his head. He slowly regained control over muscles in the top of his shoulders, arms, and hands but not on the undersides. The day he picked up a grape with his claw-like hand and managed to get it into his mouth he felt thrilled.

When Skip's neck was stable enough to allow the metal framework to be removed, he was allowed to return home. Tom Wilkins knocked out a door frame with a sledgehammer so that Skip's wheelchair could get into the downstairs room his family had converted into a bedroom for him.

"Why me?" is a question that badly injured survivors and people stricken with debilitating diseases often ask. People stricken with Parkinson's, AIDS, post-polio, cancer, spinal injuries, brain damage, cerebral palsy, amputations, blindness, and other extreme physical challenges declare, "I don't want this life!" or "I don't deserve this!" as they are forced to struggle every day to accomplish what used to be simple activities.

Skip felt depressed. His strong, well-coordinated body was gone forever; now his efforts to feed himself were clumsy. His dreams of being a star athlete in college were replaced with discouraging images of many problems he would have if he tried to attend college classes. And what girl would want to date or marry a guy stuck in a wheelchair?[1]

●　●　●　●　●　●　●　●　●　●　●　●　●

In 1985 Jackie Nink Pflug was on an Egyptian Airlines flight hijacked by terrorists. The plane ran short of fuel and landed on the island of Malta. The hijackers demanded that the plane be refueled, but local authorities refused. To force the authorities to meet their demands, the hijackers began executing passengers. Once each hour they took a passenger to the door of the plane, shot him or her in the back of the head, and threw the body down the stairs onto the runway.

Jackie Pflug was the fifth passenger shot by hijackers and thrown down the stairs. But she didn't die. She regained consciousness and almost started to move when she remembered that one of the first passengers was shot many times when she didn't die. Jackie forced herself to lay on the cold tarmac pretending to be dead.[2]

●●●●●●●●●●●●●●●●

A resilient spirit can overcome physical and emotional trauma and lead to accomplishments no one could predict. In November 1986, twenty-year-old construction worker Cliff Meidl was in a construction pit, trying to break up a concrete slab with a jackhammer. No one at the work site knew that an unmarked power line carrying thousands of volts of electricity was buried in the concrete. When the tip of his jackhammer punctured the line, 30,000 volts of electricity exploded through him. The charge was three times more powerful than that used for capital punishment in an electric chair. The explosion was so powerful it exploded out through the back of his head, his shoulder, his knee caps, and his foot and blew him out of the hole. He lay dead on the ground, his heart stopped, his clothes smoldering, his entire body singed and burned.

A firefighter quick to arrive at the scene was able to revive Cliff. His heart stopped twice more in the ambulance on the way to the hospital, but the paramedics resuscitated him each time.

He spent the next several months in the hospital while his body healed from the terrible burns. Cliff says, "I had such extensive injuries that the doctors said they would have to amputate my legs. Fortunately, one surgeon was able to save my legs with a special operation."

Cliff left the hospital in a wheelchair and began the long process of rehabilitation, which included ten more surgeries. Before his accident, he had been a runner. "I was heartbroken because the doctors said I would never walk again."

But he didn't give up. He worked hard to rebuild his strength and was eventually able to walk with braces on his legs. As part of his rehabilitation, he began to canoe and kayak. Cliff's hard work and determination led him to become one of the best kayakers in the world. He competed at the 1996

Olympic Games in Atlanta, Georgia, and qualified to represent the United States at the 2000 Olympics in Sydney, Australia.

Cliff Meidl's spirit led to him being chosen to be the United States flag bearer at the 2000 Olympic Opening Ceremonies, an honor that normally goes to returning Olympians or gold medalists. Cliff led the US athletes into the Olympic stadium in Sydney carrying the American flag. He walked proudly showing almost no sign of a limp from his damaged legs.

Cliff did not win a medal at the Olympics in Sydney, but he knows he is a winner in other ways. "The accident changed the person I am," he says. "I don't think I would have had the will and determination to make it to the Olympics without going through that experience. It made me a stronger person mentally and physically."[3]

● ● ● ● ● ● ● ● ● ● ● ● ● ●

Skip Wilkins handled his long, slow rehabilitation with good humor. As soon as possible, he resumed bass fishing, his favorite outdoor activity. With the help and support of his family, he went to college and eventually earned a degree in psychology.

At a large social gathering one evening, he watched an attractive young woman sitting and talking with some friends. He commented to his sister, "I wonder if a woman that pretty would be willing to go out with a guy like me."

His sister said, "Let's find out." She walked over to the woman, introduced herself, and said her brother wanted to ask her out on a date. Daphne, a student nurse, said she remembered Skip. They'd gone to the same high school. She'd been a freshman when he was a senior. She said she'd enjoy going out with him. Two years later they were married.

Skip decided that being in a wheelchair would not stop him from entering athletic competitions. He began a rigorous physical training program to compete in wheelchair sports. Between 1975 and 1980, he set twelve national records for wheelchair athletes in shotput, discus, precision club, and javelin. He won gold medals in many international events. He also learned to play wheelchair table tennis and won the US national wheelchair championship ten times. In 1980, he was voted the United States Athlete of the Year in Wheelchair Sports. In 1996, he served as a television co-host for the Para-Olympics in Atlanta, Georgia.

To support himself and his wife, Skip became co-owner of a company that manufactures and distributes customized work-out equipment. His pleasant manner, positive attitude toward life's challenges, and athletic achievements bring him many requests to speak. He travels around the world giving inspiring speeches to all kinds of audiences— corporate executives, prison inmates, and people challenged by physical injuries. The walls in his office and hallways are covered with photographs taken with movie stars and presidents of many countries.

Skip says his injury made him "stop competing with others and start competing with life." He emphasizes that "doing your best is a lifetime job. I would have preferred not to have my injury, but if anyone were to say they could take away my condition, I wouldn't let them if they also took away my experiences. My experiences are too rich and too wonderful to willingly give up."

By finding positive benefits in adversity, you regain control over your destiny. In the midst of experiences that you do not want and don't like, there may be aspects you do like that may turn out to be to your advantage.

The highest-level resiliency skill of all is being able to convert an extreme misfortune into a lucky event that changes your life in ways more wonderful than you ever imagined. You not only bounce back, your life is better than before. Each of us has the ability to turn negative life events into miraculous gifts if we say "Yes!" and follow the new path that suddenly opens before us.

● ● ● ● ● ● ● ● ● ● ● ● ● ●

Jackie Pflug did not move for five hours after being shot. During that time, more passengers were shot and thrown down the stairs near her. The hijackers were persuaded to allow an ambulance to come out to the plane. Jackie still played dead when the medics threw her face down onto a steel bench in the ambulance. She didn't know who the men were or where she would be taken. She continued to play possum and kept her eyes shut as they drove away from the airport. She decided she had to find out who these men were. She took a risk and asked, "Are you the good guys or the bad guys?" The medics were shocked when a woman they thought was dead suddenly spoke to them. They yelled at the driver to rush Jackie to a hospital.

Neurosurgeons removed the bullet and bone splinters from her brain, but predicted that she would be brain damaged for life. Jackie struggled to overcome her brain injury, a severe learning disability from the brain trauma, and post-traumatic stress disorder (PTSD). She had to testify at the murder trial of the hijackers. Her husband divorced her. She had to deal with bouts of depression brought on by epileptic seizures, permanent partial blindness, and no insurance to cover her huge medical bills.

Many people have been devastated by less traumatic events. Jackie, however, has recovered and rebuilt her life. She calls her recovery struggle "a grateful journey." I met her when we were on a television show together a few years ago. Jackie remarried and now has two children. Each time I see this wonderfully warm, relaxed, friendly woman, I feel awed by how resilient we humans can be.

Jackie says that to cope with her condition she had to learn to be more open, relax, listen to her inner voice, and develop a quiet inner peacefulness. She listened more and more to her inner voice. "It was an exhilarating and exciting period of growth and healing," she says. "The blinders over my eyes were being lifted, revealing a world more beautiful than I imagined."

She receives so many requests to speak to groups about coping with head injury, epilepsy, learning disabilities, and visual impairment, she has developed a career as a professional speaker. She talks to groups about using trauma as a springboard for personal growth and transformation. She says, "We are really powerless over many of the forces that shape our lives. Yet we do have power over how we respond to those situations and events."

●　●　●　●　●　●　●　●　●　●　●　●　●

My message is much like Jackie's. We are basically saying that it isn't the situation, it is how well you respond to it that counts. We are also saying that you can become better and better at handling life's adversities and be transformed by what you go through. When you are forced to cope with very distressing, life-disruptive changes, you will never be the same again. If you challenge yourself to make the heroic journey to recovery, you will spiral upward with strength instead of downward into a tailspin. You will gain new strength and emerge from your struggle a different, better person than before.

Phoenix Grievers: Families of Victims

The impact and chaos of a traumatic loss can be devastating to families of victims of terrorist attacks. They must survive, rebuild, and continue on after the agonizing loss of a loved one.

Grief counselors have assisted thousands of people through the grief process. As described by Joanne Jozefowski in her book *The Phoenix Phenomenon*, the heroic journey to rebuild a shattered life usually includes these five stages:

✦ *Impact:* shock, denial, anxiety, fear, and panic.

✦ *Chaos:* confusion, disbelief, actions out of control, irrational thoughts and feelings, feeling despair, feeling helpless, desperate searching, lose track of time, difficulty sleeping and eating, obsessive focus on the loved one and their possessions, agony from imagining their physical harm, shattered beliefs.

✦ *Adapting:* bringing order back into daily life while you continue to grieve: take care of basic needs (personal grooming, shopping, cooking, cleaning, paying bills), learn to live without the loved one, accept help, focus on helping children cope, connect with other grieving families for mutual support, take control of grieving so that grief does not control you, slowly accept the new reality.

✦ *Equilibrium:* attaining stability and routines: reestablish a life that works all right, enjoy pleasant activities with family members and good times with friends, do productive work, choose a positive new direction in life while honoring the past, learn how to handle people who ask questions about what you've been through.

+ *Transformation:* rethinking your purpose in life and the basis for your identity; looking for meaning in tragic, senseless loss; allowing yourself to have both painful and positive feelings about your loss and become able to choose which feelings you focus on; allowing yourself to discover that your struggle has led you to develop a stronger, better version of yourself than you expected could exist; learning how to talk with others about your heroic healing journey without exposing them to your pain; becoming supportive of others trying to deal with their losses.[4]

Dr. Viktor Frankl, a famous Holocaust survivor, met with many other survivors to help them overcome the loss of their loved ones. In his sessions with them, he used what he called "logotherapy." Key questions he would discuss with each person were, "If you were the one who died and your loved one was still alive, what would you wish they would be doing? What kind of life would you hope your loved one would lead if you were the one who had died?"[5]

Survivors of deadly events face many challenges. Some older veterans with a lifetime of mild PTSD symptoms experience significant increases when they see movies about their war or watch television coverage of current wars. Thousands of survivors of the September 11, 2001, terrorist attacks on the World Trade Center and the Pentagon, and the 1995 bombing of the government building in Oklahoma City, continue to feel the traumatic effects. Years after the Oklahoma City bombing, many survivors and the families of victims would feel an upsurge of old feelings each time the media reported the latest news about the court trials and sentencing of the killers. Many survivors of the terrorist attacks on the Pentagon and World Trade Center brace themselves for the ordeal they must go through every September 11 when magazines, newspapers, and television broadcasts retell what happened.

There is no medical cure for PTSD, although medications can help ease associated symptoms of depression and anxiety, and improve sleep. Sufferers can overcome their symptoms and improve their relationships in group sessions in which they relive the traumatic experience under controlled conditions, to work through the trauma until they gain control over the memories.

Survivors of repeated and prolonged trauma are not only never the same again, their trauma can be passed on to their children, thus sustaining a repeating cycle. A prime example can be found in Native Americans in the United States. A story not taught in many American history classes is that the US government and the settlers before them instigated Indian wars and mass killings of Native Americans.

Following the wars and mass killings, the US government continued a documented policy of genocide by purposefully spreading fatal diseases such as smallpox in conquered tribes. These genocidal actions reduced the original Indian population from a conservatively estimated twenty million in 1492, to about 200,000 in the 1900s.

The killings were followed by the breaking of treaties to take billions of acres of Indian lands and force Indians onto reservations. The US Bureau of Indian Affairs (BIA) systematically attempted to destroy the languages and cultures of the surviving Indians. This included removing hundreds of Indian boys and girls from their families and homelands and holding them against their will in schools run by Catholic priests and former army officers who had previously been Indian fighters. Indian children in BIA schools were punished for speaking their native languages and for having any clothing or objects representing their heritage.[7]

Present-day tribal members with college degrees in social work, counseling, and psychology have found that five centuries of historical traumas have been passed from generation to generation through oral histories and have led to multi-generational PTSD. Drs. Eduardo and Bonnie Duran, in their book, *Native American Post Colonial Psychology*, state that multi-generational PTSD continues to be at the root of many of the social, economic, physical, and spiritual ills seen in their communities today and are natural reactions to pathological situations.[8]

After centuries of US policies aimed at destroying the Native American cultures, and despite all the negative risks that Indian people still face, a revitalization is now underway—a reclaiming of traditional Indian beliefs and values. In the Pacific Northwest, for example, the region's tribes have held an annual series of "Healing the Wounded Spirit" conferences. Utilizing the traditions and spiritual practices that sustained Indian people for thousands of years, they have begun the long, slow, agonizing process of recovering from what they call their 500-year holocaust.

And they are succeeding. The 2000 census showed a population rebound to about two million. There are now many fully functioning Indian people in Indian communities. Healthcare services in tribal lands are improving. More and more Native Americans are graduating from college. At present, there are thirty-three tribal-controlled colleges—with more being built. In the years ahead, we can expect to learn much about how to survive extreme resiliency challenges from Indian people.

Each Survivor's Heroic Path to Recovery is Different

The path to recovery from deeply traumatic experiences takes many months, sometimes years. Critical-incident debriefing immediately after a tragedy has not proven to be as helpful as first hoped. Many people are not willing or able to delve into their feelings and memories for months or years.

• • • • • • • • • • • • • •

Debbie Morris was a teenage girl when she was kidnapped and raped by two men who threatened to kill her in the same way they had killed another girl. After holding her for many days, the two men released her. They were later caught, and one of them was executed for murder.

This story was made famous by the book and the movie *Dead Man Walking*. It was only after an Academy Award for the movie and widespread media attention was given to Sister Helen Prejean, the nun featured in the book and the movie, that Debbie decided to dredge up her memories and feelings of what had happened, and tell her side of the story. The outcome is that Debbie has experienced so many positive changes in her life because of what she went through, she now gives inspiring talks of hope and encouragement to many groups.[9]

* * * * * * * * * * * * * *

Jerry Schemmel was a passenger on United Airlines Flight 232 bound from Denver to Chicago when the airplane lost its steering controls. The pilots managed to keep the plane in the air and steer it in for a violent crash landing in Sioux City, Iowa. The crash tore the plane apart and set it on fire. The disaster killed 112 passengers and crew.

When the burning section of the plane that Jerry was in came to a stop, he was upside down. Jerry unbuckled his seat belt, let himself down, then helped other passengers get out through the choking smoke. He climbed out, but went back inside when he thought he heard the cry of a baby. He dug into the debris and discovered an eleven-month-old baby girl wedged into an overhead bin. He lifted the baby out, held her next to his chest inside his jacket to protect her from the dense smoke, and carried her outside. Jerry handed the baby girl to a young woman sitting on the ground, then walked into the air terminal where he washed, cleaned up, and then took the next return flight to Denver.

Back home, he did not realize at first that he was the mystery hero that had rescued the baby. He avoided media interviews and even remained a detached observer when the movie *Fearless* included a reenactment of him saving the baby.

Jerry never felt like a hero. He struggled for over seven years with survivor guilt. He couldn't get over the loss of his best friend in the crash. He went through periods of great anguish before deciding to confront his feelings and memories. He searched for help and found what he needed in the Christian church. Through much intense inner work, he finally resolved why he had been chosen to live while so many others died.[10]

The Heroic Inner Journey Back

When the survivor is ready, the nature of the heroic inner journey back to one's family and friends usually goes this way:

+ *Into the Fire: Reliving the fears and memories*
  ◇ You take the courageous step to relive your traumatic experiences with a friend, a counselor, or a support group of people who have been through similar experiences. Painful memories and feelings flood through you. You have nightmares. You feel like you are falling into a bottomless well. You find yourself reliving the experience during conversations, at movies, in a store, almost any place. You wish you'd never started this.

+ *Taking Control Phase: Wrestling for control of your spirit*
  ◇ You repeat, relive, and talk about the experience again and again with good listeners. You can call them anytime when you need their support.

+ *Transition Phase: Awkward efforts in unfamiliar territory*
  ◇ You practice telling a short version of your story to people outside your support group and circle of closest friends. You struggle with assimilating your traumatic experience into your identity. How do you deal with people who label you by your experience?

+ *Re-emerging Phase: Publicly declare and validate your new identity*
  ◇ You now control your memory of your experience; it no longer controls you. You can stop thinking about it when you want to.

  ◇ You work at making your story of your experience and your healing journey a small part of what people know about you. You avoid letting your experience become your primary identity in your own mind, even though it may be how others often refer to you.

- ✦ *Learning to Deal with Poor Listeners: Develop response choices*
  - ✧ Many who inquire about your experience are people you have to cope with. Some people ask what it was like for you, but cannot handle listening for more than a few minutes; they walk away or interrupt to express their opinions. Other people become overly sympathetic and distraught if you tell them about what you went through.

  - ✧ To handle questioners well, it is useful to develop the ability to choose to:
    a. not talk about your experience even when asked.
    b. give a short, "Reader's Digest" type of summary and then change the subject.
    c. talk in detail with the rare person who is sincerely interested, will take time to listen, and is a good listener.

- ✦ *Speaking with Wisdom, Not Pain: The process works*
  - ✧ You discover at times that you've gone many days without thinking of the painful experience or your long healing journey. You appreciate that your emotional wounds have healed, that you are free from what happened, and that your recovery struggle has changed you into a better person than you were before. Family and friends enjoy being with you. Your wise advice is sought by others.

The Long Struggle from "Before" to a Good Life "After"

Elia Zedeño was working on the 73rd floor of the North Tower in the World Trade Center (WTC) on September 11, 2001. She got out of the building fast when the alarms went off. She knew how deadly a terrorist attack could be. She had been trapped in an elevator in the WTC in February, 1993, when a truck bomb set off in the central parking garage killed six people and injured over 1,000. "When I expressed my fears to others about another attack," she says, "most co-workers responded with, 'lightning never strikes the same place twice.' I wasn't so sure but, distracted by my duties at work, I slowly forgot the incident and went about as if nothing had ever happened."

On 9/11, Elia escaped from the North Tower unharmed, but says, "I spent many days crying in front of the television set, watching in disbelief at what had become of the place where I loved working for over twenty years. My house never emptied of family and concerned friends, yet I felt very much alone."

Elia worked in the WTC headquarters offices of The Port Authority of New York and New Jersey. She says, "If we did not regroup quickly, many companies stood to experience financial hardship and even bankruptcy, along with their employees. We relocated to a Port Authority facility in Jersey City, New Jersey, right away. The idea of the message it would send if terrorism tore down a country's financial stability was my driving force behind getting back to work quickly. I felt this was a most needed contribution, where I could do my best with the knowledge and skills I have.

"I was in charge of maintaining a database that contained all our files. Since the database was created after the 1993 event, I had insisted it be backed up outside the WTC site. Shortly after 9/11, I regained access to it in the new facility. I'd love to say it was all smooth sailing from this point on, but it seemed that it was only the beginning of the end for me.

"In February of 2002," she says, "I was fully engrossed in my work. I believed there was no time for tears and fearful thoughts. There was also no time for, or thoughts of, God. I developed an increasingly serious sore throat and symptoms of a cold including a high fever and throat infection. In April I was taken from work to the hospital by ambulance."

After she recovered, Elia went to see a counselor. She says, "I felt helpless and out of control. My main objective was to arrive at a point where I could recall the experiences of 9/11 without getting emotional. The counselor had me list what was wrong with my life in every area—spiritual, psychological, social, and professional."

Her lists were long.

"At the spiritual level, I questioned the purpose of my being and my survival. I could not bring myself to read spiritual books, pray, or write in my journal. I could not offer sincere words of comfort to others. I felt a sense of hopelessness and meaninglessness.

"At the psychological level, I felt overwhelmed by sadness, despair, and foreboding. I felt sorry for myself. I felt lonely and depressed. I wished I was among the ones who perished, in a desperate attempt to escape from the agony of remembering. I felt guilty for having survived. I felt tortured by my thoughts and memories. I felt tortured by my imagination. I imagined how certain people died; their horrible experiences. I felt lost and disoriented. I felt a sense of peril for the future. And I hated myself for not being strong enough to overcome.

"At the social level, I was increasingly alienated from friends, family, and pets. I locked myself in my room on weekends. I was 'sick and tired' of being told I was strong. I wanted to disappear. I missed my co-workers who had perished. I missed the buildings.

"At the professional level, I had many negative and irrational reactions to issues at work. I took things personally and saw others as aggressors. I wanted to go back in time. I cried on and off at work.

"And finally, I was angry in myself for feeling all of the symptoms and for having returned to the towers after the 1993 ordeal. After all, I regarded myself as intelligent enough to know better and resilient enough to overcome on my own. Since I was set in believing I alone could prevail, it stressed me to think I was struggling."

Elia says, "It took many months to reach a sense of reawakening to a familiar yet new level of consciousness. On the one-year anniversary of the attack, I attended a memorial service. There, I forced myself to look at the New York skyline where the towers had been."

Upon returning home, she wrote the following:

One September morning they left without warning. On the
wings of war my beloved twins departed. Their flight was difficult.
My twins invited me on their journey. They told me many
would join them, but I declined. I still hear them beckoning me to
follow them, but still I decline.
One year later I say good-bye to my tall friends and I bid
farewell to all who traveled with them.

Through writing and talking with others, Elia says her
pain "was gradually replaced with positive thoughts about
my experiences and about myself. A form of clarity has
emerged and freedom to choose became a reality. Today I find
myself asking who I am in comparison to an experience. Then
I ask myself whom do I choose to be in the moment. Upon
recalling my desperate attempts to forget the past, I see now the
point is not in forgetting but accepting the event as part of my
history. The experience itself is not who I am but what made me,
as it is not the 'crucifixion' that counts, but the 'resurrection.'"

Two years after the 9/11 tragedy, Elia and a close co-
worker who is also a 9/11 survivor formed a meditation and
book-study group where all are welcome to attend. Elia
joined a Toastmasters club to improve her ability to speak
about what she has learned and experienced.

"Currently," she says, "I welcome and enjoy spending
time with friends, family, co-workers, and pets. I have chosen
to take responsibility for every chapter in my life, on a personal and professional level. Where once I saw misfortune,
today I see only opportunities for growth in me. Anger has
turned to a thankfulness that has moved me to a new level of
understanding.

"Once I struggled to return to a time and place prior to 9/
11, I even struggled to be who I was. Yet one morning I awoke
to find myself leaving behind whom I once was and welcoming an entirely new person. The uplifting sensation is alive in
me even now upon recalling the moment.

"Neale Donald Walsch, author of the *Conversations With
God* book series, said it best during an interview. He stated,

'When your life feels as if it's falling apart, it may just be falling together for the first time.'"[11]

Transformed into a Stronger and Better Person

Elia, like many who have made the long, heroic journey fighting their way back through extreme terror, survival panic, and ghastly memories, did more than recover. She is like many others who emerge transformed. It's unexpected after feeling lost and helpless in a swamp of painful feelings, memories, and fears for so long.[12]

And along with the new feeling comes more compassion, love, and strength. Such survivors often feel compelled to make themselves available to others who haven't completed their resiliency journey yet. Three years after being a 9/11 survivor, Elia registered with September Space, a self-organized center for WTC survivors, to become a volunteer for helping other survivors.

* * * * * * * * * * * * * *

Richard Williams is a survivor of the 1995 bombing of the Murrah building in Oklahoma City. His office was on the ground-floor level near where the truck exploded. A thick cement wall imploded on him, and the ceiling fell on him, ripping off his left ear. Cement, wood, glass, office furniture, and other rubble from above crashed down, completely burying him. In the confusion, no one knew he was alive under the mounds of debris. Hours later a fireman discovered him, pulled him out, and carried him to an ambulance.

Richard was the building-operations manager. He knew most of the 169 people killed in the blast. As soon as his injuries allowed, he began working to help the blast survivors, families of victims, rescue workers, and others whose lives were changed forever to create a lasting memorial to those who were lost.

Ken Thompson lost his mother in the bombing. Ken says that losing her in such a horrible, senseless way was a deep shock to him. Instead of withdrawing and dwelling on his loss, however, he volunteered to work on the memorial project. Ken says, "Until that time, my only purpose in life was to earn enough money as an assistant manager at a credit union to have a nice car and enjoy the life of a bachelor. Losing my mother made me look at what is really important in my life. I went to all the community meetings to contribute what I could."

Ken, Richard, and many others worked long hard months to influence and create a suitable memorial. In the process, they started asking, "Is there any way we can help other communities avoid having to go through this?" The outcome was the creation of the International Center for the Prevention of Terrorism, with Ken Thompson as its first director.

Ken says, "The tragedy changed me. Now I get up each morning with two goals. One is to live the day such that my mother would be proud of me. The other goal is to be useful to others who are struggling with recovering from terrorist attacks." Ken has traveled to Ireland, Palestine, Iraq, and many other places to speak and provide model plans for preventing terrorist attacks.

Soon after the WTC tragedy, Ken, Richard, and a few others from Oklahoma City flew to New York at their own expense and provided valuable assistance to survivors, families of victims, and rescue workers. An instant bond was made with the New York fire and rescue workers, because New York city sent a rescue team to Oklahoma City immediately after the bombing in 1995. Part of the WTC tragedy was that nine of the firefighters who had been in Oklahoma City were killed when the towers collapsed.

Ken and Richard have been helpful in talking with survivors and families of victims in New York, because the survivors and families of victims in Oklahoma City made an early commitment to be supportive of each other and work together. A problem that follows killings by terrorists is that some families, in their grief, will be angry at survivors and try to exclude them from recovery resources and memorial activities. People experiencing deep grief and loss will sometimes say and do things they later regret—but that's all right. These are human reactions and can be overcome.[13]

Three years after the 9/11 tragedy, Ken, Richard, and one of Richard's co-workers flew to New York to participate in a gathering of survivors, families of victims, and rescue workers. They brought with them a sapling from the Oklahoma City "survivor tree." An American Elm tree in a parking lot across the street from the Murrah building was blasted by shrapnel and set on fire by the bomb explosion. All fall and winter it looked dead. But in the spring, new leaves sprouted as work was progressing across the street to prepare the memorial site. It became a symbol of community resiliency, and now saplings grown from its seeds are being given to survivor groups all over the world.

• • • • • • • • • • • • • • •

It has been almost a century since Nietschze made people aware that they not only have the ability to endure and recover from torturous experiences, but can emerge stronger and better than they were before. The heroic resiliency journey back from extreme trauma and tragedy is rough, has setbacks, and is different for every person, family, and community. Recovery is possible, however, and transformation into a life that is better after the tragedy than it was before is often an unexpected outcome.

In recent years, a few psychologists have observed what they call post-traumatic growth (PTG).[14] Their work is contributing to the emerging new field of positive psychology in which many psychologists are finding that the mental-illness concepts in psychiatry are counterproductive to promoting resiliency.[15]

My resiliency research has created in me a profound appreciation of the ability of people to heal from extreme injuries and life-shattering experiences, and emerge from their struggle changed in ways that they value. We are born with the ability to be transformed by experiences so extreme they change us forever.

We have the ability to draw meaning and value out of horrible experiences. Painful memories can be neutralized by finding gifts in the experience. The search for inner peace can bring depth of understanding, compassion, and wisdom. Trauma can lead to wisdom and become a door to a new and fulfilling life.

Resiliency Development Activity

▶ Talk with survivors who have been through incredibly difficult experiences and are happy, pleasant people. Find out for yourself how survivors of extreme adversities are able to be happy and free of bitterness.

A benefit you gain from interviewing survivors is that you feel the effect of their presence and energy. Notice how you feel after an interview. What is it about survivors transformed by adversity that makes them different from most other people?

Chapter Thirteen

Our Transformational Breakthrough

A 5,000-Year-Old Insight

The *I Ching,* known in the Western world as *The Book of Changes,* is the oldest continuously used book in human history. Its origin traces back almost 5,000 years. The title, in Chinese characters, expresses three meanings. It communicates that (1) change is constant, (2) change is the only stable reference point in life, and (3) the never-ending process of change can be simple, easy, and natural for us.[1]

Chinese sages were not the only observers of the constancy of change. Around 500 BC, the Greek philosopher Heraclitus founded a school of philosophy based on his observation that "all things change," including all humans.[2]

It fascinates me to find that Chinese sages and Greek philosophers understood and taught a message thousands of years ago that is so relevant today. Each of us lives in a constantly changing environment. We can make our lives difficult by denying, resisting, or fighting against the ongoing process of change, or we can adapt and flow with changes; it's our choice. By accepting that unceasing change permeates our lives and that many kinds of energy constantly swirl through and around us, we can free ourselves from being buffeted around like leaves in a storm. When we choose to flow along with the energies of change, we can often get good outcomes by choosing when to act or not act in certain ways. Our inborn ability to keep learning new ways of interacting with the world can lead us to learn how to navigate through rough times of change so skillfully ...that we can enjoy the journey.

Why Isn't Everyone Resilient?

Two puzzling questions lurked on the edge of my research for a long time: If humans have an inborn predisposition to learn how to become more and more resilient as they interact with the world, why do so many people feel distressed and over-whelmed by the current churn of change? Why do so many people need classes and coaching on how to be resilient in turbulent times?

When I searched for answers, I found that many adults had their inborn resiliency abilities stunted during childhood. They were trained to fit into a slow-to-change world where disruptive change was infrequent, temporary, and resolved by the authorities in charge.

In recent times, as a consequence, the experiential world of many people has changed from being stable and safe to being unstable, with unpredictable, life-disrupting change. For a person raised to fit into an unchanging world, the changes can feel unfair. Unceasing, disruptive change can devastate the finances, relationships, and health of people who do not cope well.

A positive outcome of the current turmoil is that more and more people raised to be cooperative "good children" are breaking free from constricting emotional fetters to discover they have inborn resiliency abilities they did not know they had. People are freeing their minds from the consensus reality about stress. More people are now questioning what experts and authorities tell them to do.

Becoming a Highly Resilient Human Being

As I learned more and more about highly resilient people, I began to sense a dynamic, complex, energy pattern in what I was observing. I listed many signs that people are being forced by current conditions to transform from a less effective way of being to a new, more effective way of being. The transformation includes these changes:

From:	*To:*
resisting change	embracing change
acting "good"	interacting synergistically
being well trained	self-managed learning
a scripted personality	a discovered personality
self-depreciation	self-appreciation
acting as one should	doing what works well
living by appearances	living by the feel of things
constructed realities	discovered realities
fixed procedures	ongoing processes
being	becoming
socially compliant	social involvement
"I win, you lose"	"We all win"
obedient cooperation	cooperative nonconformity
acting morally	living morally
dependent or independent	interdependent
job descriptions	professionalism
rules	values, principles, and ethics
managing with statements	managing with questions
judgmental thinking	validating empathy
emotional stupidity	emotional intelligence
needing demeaned opposites	independent identity
external locus of control	internal locus of control
rigid or weak boundaries	strong, permeable boundaries
act one way	complex, paradoxical responses
(selfish or unselfish)	(selfish unselfishness)
unthinking reacting	conscious responding with choices (either/or; to do/not do; both/and)
following role instructions	author of one's life story
controlling the environment	in harmony with environment
stress	resiliency
post traumatic stress disorder	post traumatic growth

These lists demonstrate the depth and breadth of the transformation in progress. The changes are extensive, pervasive, and profound.

But while I could see many indicators of a profound transformation taking place, my intuitive sense of pattern empathy kept signaling to me that I was still missing an important insight. I wondered: What is it that I don't see yet? I see many trees, but not the forest. Why has the field of psychology taken so long to start trying to understand resiliency? Why has there been such a dearth of language and concepts in the field of psychology for describing the unique, complex, synergistic nature of resilient people?

Scientific Reductionism Handicapped Psychology

A review of the origins of psychology revealed some answers. In the late 1800s, the first psychologists, led by Wilhelm Wundt, tried to prove that psychology was a legitimate science by adopting two predominant beliefs in the established sciences. First, that the human mind functions independently from the human body—something like the way a speech recorded on a cassette tape is independent from the tape it is recorded on.

Second, that all objects and the movements of objects could be understood by *reducing* them into their component parts and functions. This view was first described in the late 1600s by Isaac Newton, who asserted that all moving objects moved in mechanistic ways determined by certain laws and principles. His brilliant explanation of gravity (said to be an outcome of being hit on the head by a falling apple) persuaded scientists and mathematicians to accept that all events in the world are determined by laws of cause and effect, and that all of nature could eventually be understood by *scientific reductionism.*

Thus it was that the first psychology researchers believed that scientific reductionism was the only valid way to study human beings. The researchers viewed people as things, as objects for study, as they tried to reduce all human behaviors into simple, mechanistic principles. They developed scientific methods for conducting experiments performed on their "subjects." They examined and dissected people's brains, nervous systems, sensory receptors, emotions, and motivations to identify the basic structures that explain human behavior. Research that could not be replicated in laboratories was deemed not valid.

Personality researchers developed techniques for categorizing and labeling people according to core traits the researchers looked for. Psychologists searched for factors that determine human development and studied how people acquire learned behavior. The leading proponents of behaviorism, Ivan Pavlov and B. F. Skinner, asserted that animal and human behavior results from "stimulus-response" conditioning and reinforcements.

Freud created a new way of analyzing the mental and emotional lives of people with a method he called psychoanalysis. He claimed that infantile feelings and memories influence an adult's thoughts, feelings, and actions. He said that unconscious defense mechanisms distort how every person thinks, feels, and perceives others. *Freudianism* led mainstream psychiatrists and clinical psychologists into seeing symptoms of mental illness in almost everyone. When they found what they were looking for, they took that as proof that Freud's theories were valid.

For most of its first 100 years, the field of psychology was permeated by scientific reductionism. Ironically, even though the term "psychology" means "the study of the human soul" (from the Latin word "psyche"), psychologists excluded "soul" from their studies.

Scientific reductionism in psychology was enhanced by the invention of large computers that could run huge computational programs capable of "factor analysis." Psychologists consumed millions of key-punched computer cards in their efforts to identify core human motives, attitudes, and personality structures. Throughout all of this, psychologists erroneously believed they were detached, objective observers of the determinants of human behavior. Their identity as scientists included believing that whatever they observed in human and animal behavior was objective, impersonally and unemotionally observed information, free of subjective influences.

Behaviorism and Freudianism dominated the field of psychology for many decades. In 1954, Abraham Maslow provided a more *humane* and validating way of understanding people, when he published his book *Motivation and Personality*. He argued that psychologists should study positive aspects of people's lives and work to understand self-actualized people.[3] But *humanistic* psychology, sometimes called the "third wave," was never accepted by mainstream psychologists committed to using scientific, reductionistic research methods.

Scientific reductionism allowed psychologists to gain valuable knowledge about human behavior. As can be seen in any introductory psychology textbook, scientific methods led to many discoveries about why people act, think, and feel the way they do. But until recent times, psychology researchers did not see that the thoughts, feelings, and actions of the most life-competent people cannot be understood without understanding the circumstances each individual person is interacting with—from his or her point of view.

I'm not saying that scientific reductionism in psychology was wrong. It wasn't. But I believe that now it is necessary to add a fresh new way of understanding how people become highly skilled at interacting effectively with constantly changing circumstances.

As I've stated several times, my education in psychology was often more of a handicap than an asset in my efforts to understand highly resilient individuals. It never felt right to me that most psychology theories reduced people into categories, and that the theory was bigger than each person described. I never found a psychological theory that conceptualized any person studied as being psychologically bigger and more complex than the theory.

Freed By the Uncertainty Principle

It delighted me to find that my understanding of highly resilient survivors is validated by perspectives developed by scientists in other fields. Physicists doing basic research into the structure of matter discovered that solid matter is mostly space. When scientific reductionism is used to investigate physical matter, physicists find no solid particles underlying the structure of any objects we experience as solid.[4] What we perceive as solid matter is actually an assemblage of innumerable, minuscule energy potentials vibrating in relation to each other at incredible speeds. All matter, it turns out, is made up of self-organized strings of energy potentials.[5]

The term "potential" is important to understand. Werner Heisenberg's revolutionary discovery in physics was called the Uncertainty Principle because the nature of what will be observed has only a *potential* form before an observation occurs. The observations and measurements made by researchers affect what is being observed. If a researcher sets up equipment to find subatomic *particles*, he or she will find particles. If a researcher sets up equipment to find *electrical charges*, he or she will find electrical charges. Researchers find what they set out to find.

Heisenberg's Uncertainty Principle established that a detached objective observation or measurement from outside a subatomic system is not possible. The act of observing affects what is observed. This makes the observer an influencing factor in the system under study. The system cannot be fully understood without examining the observer's intentions and measuring methods.[6]

How does this relate to understanding resiliency? In two significant ways.

First, highly resilient people are present in situations with many potential behaviors available for quick use. What they will do, feel, or say does not exist until they are engaged in a situation. What they will do cannot be predicted in advance.

Traditional psychology was based on the belief that scientifically valid tests could identify an individual's personality traits and that the same traits would be seen whenever the person was observed or tested. Resiliency psychology asserts that while that may be true for individuals who impose a predetermined way of acting or thinking in most situations, the actions and behaviors of resilient people in any situation will reflect the nature of the situation. In addition, chance factors, past experience, and/or playfulness may mean that a resilient person will act much differently than he or she did previously in the same situation.

Second, psychologists and psychiatrists have not studied how their expectations influenced the person or people being studied. When clinical psychologists and psychiatrists looked for signs of mental illness, emotional trauma, or impairment, they found illness, trauma, and impairment.

Mainstream psychologists are only recently beginning to discover that when they look with positive expectations for good coping skills, resiliency, and post traumatic growth, they find what they look for. It's been in people all the time, but reports of such abilities were dismissed as anecdotal stories because the abilities could not be replicated in scientifically controlled settings.

Resiliency-psychology research is opening psychologists to seeing a new, validating way of viewing how humans respond to adversity. Resiliency research is revealing the existence of a way of being human that cannot be comprehended by traditional, scientific, reductionistic methods.

How Complex, Self-Organizing Systems Are Formed

Biologists discovered long ago that the chromosomes in a fertilized egg do not carry a final and complete, unchanging blueprint of the body that will ultimately develop. They're just a starting point. As the cells in the embryo multiply and differentiate, newly emerging cells act as though they already "know" what functions have been assumed by the differentiated cells that came before them. This "knowledge" causes them to become different types of cells as needed to build the final form. Embryonic development is influenced more by the morphogenic field of its future complete body than by the physical structure of its chromosomes.[7]

Ilya Prigogine was awarded a Nobel prize in 1977 for research proving that certain phenomena in chemistry did not fit with Newton's universal, reductionistic laws. Prigogine's experiments revealed the following:

1. If the energy input increases beyond what a closed, simple system can withstand or absorb, the system's structure becomes disorganized and fluctuates in chaotic ways. It reaches what Prigogine called a "bifurcation point," and "When we come close to bifurcation points, the fluctuations become abnormally high." The system will either disintegrate, or it will reorganize into a more complex, open, nonlinear system able to absorb, process, and dissipate the higher energy levels.

2. Systems do not change from simple, closed forms into complex, open forms in a predictable, determined, linear, step-by-step process. Prigogine found that the living systems developed their structures in unpredictable nonlinear ways. He concluded that complex living systems self-organize with internal structures that harmonize with the energies they take in and process. What the new order will be like cannot be predicted using traditional linear, deterministic principles because "local events have repercussions throughout the entire system."

3. Open, nonlinear, complex systems need disequilibrium or they will deteriorate. He described a simple, closed system in equilibrium as "blind" to outside events. In contrast, he found that an open, complex system exists in "far-from-equilibrium conditions." It "is able to perceive, to 'take into account' in its way of functioning, differences in the external world" and will become "adapted to outside conditions."[8]

Highly Resilient, Uniquely Complex, Self-Forming Humans

Heisenberg's and Prigogine's findings match the resiliency principles and processes described in this book in two ways:

First, you become highly resilient by continuously learning your best way of being yourself in your circumstances. You develop your own unique version of resiliency through a teleological process.[9] This explains why reductionistic "seed" or "root causes" psychological theories of healthy psychological development are so inadequate.

Second, when external demands exceed what your old habits and ways of coping are able to handle, you will be driven to a bifurcation point—a moment in your life where you will never be the same again. It is here that a breakdown may not be a bad thing. If you can avoid being crushed beyond recovery, and do your best to resile, the outcome will be that you can emerge from the experience a different, better, and more effective person. Changes in how your brain and mind function can take place at any age. Psychologists have recently discovered that the human brain can remain plastic in its ability to reorganize throughout one's lifetime.[10]

When you use the new knowledge about the many interwoven connections between your physical body and what you think and feel, you can maintain optimal health and energy through long periods of difficult challenges. When you allow previously unused, inner capacities to develop, you become stronger, more complex, wiser, and more skilled at handling future similar situations should they occur again.

The Uncertainty Principle can be observed in highly resilient people—if we look. Highly resilient, synergistic people can choose from many combinations of thinking and responding. They can be optimistic and/or pessimistic, self-motivated and/or compliant, task oriented and/or relationship oriented. They can choose to be both one way and another, or either one way or another, in many dimensions of thinking and feeling.

Most times, however, resilient people just quietly do what they do. Their various, numerous, counterbalanced ways of being are *potential* states. Their ability to engage in positivity and/or negativity, for example, remains unactivated until a situation brings out either or both dimensions.

Psychiatrist Robert Jay Lifton created the term "protean" to describe people whose form changes according to the situations they are in. He derived the word "protean" from Proteus, the Greek sea god able to take many forms. Lifton says the protean person searches for a form of self that has authenticity and meaning: "The protean self seeks to be both fluid and grounded, however tenuous that combination. There is nothing automatic about the enterprise...but rather a continuous effort without clear termination. Proteanism, then, is a balancing act between responsive shapeshifting, on the one hand, and efforts to consolidate and cohere, on the other."[11]

Prigogine's discovery of the importance of disequilibrium to complex systems applies to resilient people as well. At a time when many people yearn to return to a life of stability, constancy, and little change, it seems almost irrational to accept that a complex living system needs a constant state of disequilibrium if it is to function in an optimal way. For humans, this means that constant change is necessary and desirable. No change and little activity lead to deterioration. Further, chaotic disequilibrium creates an opportunity for a living system to spontaneously "self-reorganize" into a different, complex energy system that is better suited for the world it exists in.[12] This perspective confirms my observation that highly resilient people keep getting better and better because they go through life interacting with the world like curious children.

The struggle to deal with nonstop change in the business world is pressuring corporations to change their business models. A few are integrating resiliency processes and the principles of self-organizing systems into their operations.[13] This is another reason why resilient people are best suited for employment in a world of nonstop change.

An Old/New Way of Being

Highly complex, resilient, synergistic individuals are always curious, exploring, trying new ways of doing things, and learning. They maintain mental and emotional stability by keeping themselves in a state of mild disequilibrium. They are open to take in, examine, and process new inputs, ignore or let go what is not of value or interest, and move on to the next experience. Thus it is that they become accustomed to quickly taking in and processing new things that are happening. They can react to an unexpected, life-disrupting change by welcoming it and converting it into a desirable life event.

The findings from modern physics, the teachings of ancient sages, and the new resiliency psychology all fit together. We are born able to learn how to handle nonstop, disruptive change easily and naturally, and constant change is necessary and desirable for us as humans. We are most resilient when we scan new circumstances with curiosity, not knowing in advance what we will do, but confident that we will interact in ways that lead to things working well.

Resiliency Development Activity

▶ What advantages do you see in allowing yourself to enter new situations not knowing what you will do?

Notes

Preface

1. We've been in an era in which mental health professionals assumed and insisted that every person who has gone through a horrendous experience must be emotionally traumatized. A few mental health professionals have only recently come to the realization that about eighty percent of people experiencing emotional trauma are so resilient they can overcome the experience without therapy or treatment. See: Gladwell, Malcolm. "Getting Over It." *The New Yorker,* November 8, 2004, pp. 75–79. Also see: Bonanno, George A. "Loss, Trauma, and Resilience: Have We Underestimated the Human Capacity to Thrive After Extremely Aversive Events?" *American Psychologist,* January, 2004, Vol. 59, No. 1, pp. 20–28.

2. "Mental illness" and "mental health" are hypothetical constructs–they are professional opinions that require a licensed psychiatrist or clinical psychologist to determine. In contrast, "survivor personality" and "highly resilient person" are abstracted systems. They are descriptions of patterns of actions, feelings, and thoughts that can be observed and verified by anyone. See: Maddux, James E. "Stopping the Madness: Positive Psychology and the Deconstruction of the Illness Ideology and the DSM." *Handbook of Positive Psychology,* C. R. Snyder and Shane J. Lopez, eds. (New York: Oxford University Press, 2002).

3. Maslow, Abraham. *Eupsychian Management.* (Homewood, IL: Irwin & Dorsey Press, 1965) p. 76.

Chapter 1. Thriving in Today's World

1. Cynthia Dailey-Hewkin story, personal interviews.

2. Hamel, Gary, and Liisa Välikangas. "The Quest for Resilience." *Harvard Business Review,* September, 2003, p. 52.

3. Tranquilizer addiction data from the National Institute on Drug Abuse. Website: www.DrugAbuse.gov/ResearchReports/ (accessed September 27, 2004).

4. Frankl,Viktor. *Man's Search For Meaning* (first published by Beacon Press, 1956. Reissued by Washington Square Press, 1985), p. 103.

5. Job loss e-mail exchange at www.ResiliencyCenter.com, August 18–19, 2004.

6. Armstrong, Lance. *It's Not About the Bike* (New York: Berkley Publishing Group, 2001). Also, quotes from broadcast interviews and his website, www.LanceArmstrong.com

Chapter 3. How Resilient Are You?

1. Gert Boyle story from the Columbia Sportswear newspaper articles and www.ColumbiaSportswear.com website (accessed July, 2004).
2. The internal/external self-assessment used here is adapted from Rotter, Julian. "External and Internal Control." *Psychology Today*, June, 1971.
3. Deci, Edward and Robert Ryan. *Intrinsic Motivation and Self-Determination in Human Behavior* (New York: Plenum Press, 1985).
4. Harris, Bill. *Thresholds of Mind: How Holsync Audio Technology Can Transform Your Life* (Beaverton, OR: Centerpointe Research Institute, 2002); Also, personal interviews, and Centerpointe Research Institute, 4720 S.W. Washington Street, Suite 104, Beaverton, OR 97005. Website: www.Centerpointe.com.
5. Suzy Kellett story, personal interviews.
6. Tom Kelley story, personal interviews. A lawsuit brought by stockholders against the Resolution Trust has been adjudicated in their favor.
7. Siebert, Al. *Resiliency: An Essential Skill in a Rapidly Changing Workplace* and *The Resiliency Manual for Public Employees* (Portland, OR: Practical Psychology Press, 2002).
8. Adams, Marilee G. *Change Your Questions, Change Your Life: 7 Powerful Tools for Life and Work* (San Francisco: Berrett-Koehler, 2004).

Chapter 4. Optimize Your Health (Level 1)

1. Selye, Hans. *The Stress of My Life: A Scientist's Memoirs*, 2nd edition (New York: Van Nostrand Reinhold, 1979), p. 78.
2. For a typical example of an article spreading the myth of stress, see: "Job Stress May Be Killing You." *Discover* magazine, December 2003, p. 17.
3. The General Adaptation Syndrome is described in many books. See: Selye, Hans. *Stress of My Life*.
4. Vahtera, Jussi, et al. "Organizational Downsizing, Sickness Absence, and Mortality: A 10 Town Perspective Cohort Study." *British Medical Journal*, February 23, 2004.
5. Diener, Ed, Richard E. Luca, and Shigehiro Oishi. "Subjective Well-Being: The Science of Happiness and Life Satisfaction." *Handbook of Positive Psychology*, C. R. Snyder and Shane J. Lopez, eds. (New York: Oxford University Press, 2002).

6. Workshops conducted for US civil service personnel, Naval Air Station, Jacksonville, Florida, January, 2000.

7. Smith, Joshua M., and James W. Pennebaker. "Sharing One's Story: Translating Emotional Experiences into Words as a Coping Tool." *Coping: The Psychology of What Works*, C. R. Snyder, ed. (New York: Oxford Press, 1999).

8. Illinois Bell story at www.BellSystemMemorial.com/att_divestiture.html (accessed September 18, 2003).

9. Maddi, Salvatore R. and Susan C. Kobasa. *The Hardy Executive: Health Under Stress* (New York: Dow-Jones Irwin, 1984). For an update on the hardiness research, see: Maddi, Salvadore R. "The Story of Hardiness: Twenty Years of Theorizing, Research, and Practice." *Consulting Psychology Journal*, 2002, Vol. 54, pp. 173–185. Online: www.PsychologyMatters.org/hardiness.html (accessed January, 2005).

10. Chambers, Harry. *My Way Or the Highway.* (San Francisco: Berrett-Koehler, 2004). Contains excellent tips on how to handle a manager who micromanages.

11. Cohen, Sheldon. "Social Relationships and Health," in *American Psychologist*, November, 2004, Vol. 59, No. 8, pp. 676–684.

12. Glasser, William. *Positive Addiction* (New York: Harper, 1976).

13. Charnofsky, Stan. "Suicide by Lifestyle." *AHP Perspective*, August/September, 2004, pp. 11–13. For one of the first comprehensive reports about lifestyle habits that shorten people's lives see: Matarazzo, Joseph. "Behavioral Health's Challenge to Academic, Scientific, and Professional Psychology." *American Psychologist*, January, 1982, pp. 1–14. Also see: Siebert, Al. *The Survivor Personality* (New York: Perigee, 1996), p. 159.

14. Seligman, Martin E. P., and Mihaly Csikszentmihalyi, eds. "Special Issue on Happiness, Excellence, and Optimal Human Functioning." *American Psychologist*, January, 2000.

15. "How to Live to Be 100." *Time* magazine, August 30, 2004, pp. 40–48.

16. "The Power of Rest: Revive Yourself by Doing Nothing." *Utne* magazine feature stories, January–February, 2004, pp. 76–85.

17. Benson, Herbert, and William Proctor. *Beyond the Relaxation Response* (New York: Berkley Publishing Group, 1994).

18. Glasser, William. The Ten Axioms of Choice Theory." *Choice Theory: A New Psychology of Personal Freedom* (New York: HarperCollins, 1998), pp. 332–336.

Chapter 5. Skillfully Problem Solve (Level 2)

1. Richard S. Lazarus. *Emotion and Adaptation* (New York: Oxford University Press, 1961).
2. Mary Steinhardt's resiliency research reported in: Aitken, Sandi, and John Morgan. "How Motorola Promotes Good Health." *The Journal for Quality and Participation,* Jan/Feb, 1999, pp. 54–57.
3. Stanton, Annette L., and Robert Franz. "Focusing On Emotion: An Adaptive Coping Strategy?" *Coping: The Psychology of What Works,* C. R. Snyder, ed. (New York: Oxford University Press, 1999).
4. Snyder, C. R., and Beth L. Dinoff. "Coping: Where Have You Been?" *Ibid.,* pp. 9–10. Also see: Salovey, Peter, et al. "Coping Intelligently: Emotional Intelligence and the Coping Process." *Ibid,* pp. 141–164.
5. Frederickson, Barbara L. "Positive Emotion." *Handbook of Positive Psychology,* C. R. Snyder and Shane J. Lopez, eds. (New York: Oxford University Press, 2002). Also see: Isen, Alice M. "Positive Affect as a Source of Human Strength." *In A Psychology of Human Strengths,* Lisa G. Aspinwall and Ursula M. Staudinger, eds. (Washington, DC: American Psychological Association, 2003).
6. Sternberg, Robert J. "Culture and Intelligence." *American Psychologist,* July/August, 2004. Vol. 59, No. 5, pp. 325–338.
7. Dan Wilk story from personal interviews. Rubber-band balls have been around for decades. Wilk's patent is a design patent for a rubber-band ball with a wide outside band that carries a printed message on it. Bandyball® is enjoying sustained success because of free advertising-such as the TV ad run by OfficeMax during a Super Bowl game. The Bandyball offices are located in Northbrook, Illinois, and still contracts work with Opportunity, Inc. Roger Wilk, Dan's father, is the CEO.
8. Archimedes legendary discovery, *The Columbia Encyclopedia,* 3rd edition (New York: Columbia University Press, 1963).
9. Wiseman, Richard. *The Luck Factor: Changing Your Luck, Changing Your Life-The Four Essential Principles* (New York: Miramax Books, 2003).
10. Psychologist Sarnoff Mednick developed the Remote Associations Test at the University of Michigan in the 1960s. His copyrighted version has high validity.
11. Buzan, Tony. *The Mind Map Book: How to Use Radiant Thinking to Utilize Your Brain's Untapped Potential* (New York: E.P. Dutton, 1994).

12. Keyes, Ken, Jr. *Taming Your Mind* (Coos Bay, OR: Love Line Books, 1975).
13. Mensa story told at a Mensa meeting, October, 1993.

Chapter 6. Strengthen Inner Selfs (Level 3)

1. Siebert, Al. "The Roots of Resiliency: Your Inner Selfs." *The Survivor Personality* (New York: Perigee, 1996), pp. 143–153. Draws on and expands the information in *TSP* chapter 12.
2. For an in-depth perspective of the ways that well-meaning parents instill ways of thinking and feeling in their children that become emotional handicaps later in life, read "The Good-Child Handicap," *ibid.*, chapter 8.
3. White, Robert W. "Motivation Reconsidered: The Concept of Competence." *Psychological Review*, Vol. 66, September, 1959, pp. 297–333.
4. Bandura, Albert. *Self-Efficacy: The Exercise of Control* (New York: Freeman, 1997). Also see: Maddux, James E. "Self-Efficacy: The Power of Believing You Can." *Handbook of Positive Psychology*, C. R. Snyder and Shane J. Lopez, eds. (New York: Oxford University Press, 2002).
5. Reeve, Christopher. *Still Me* (New York: Random House, 1998), p. 275.
6. Murphy, John T. *Success Without a College Degree* (Seattle: Achievement Dynamics, Inc., 2001), pp. ix–x.
7. John Mitchell story, personal interviews.
8. Crocker, J., and B. Major. "Social Stigma and Self-Esteem: The Self-protective Properties of Stigma." *Psychological Review*, 1989, vol. 96, pp. 608–630.
9. Pendlum, David. *So, Who Do You Think You Are?* (Chesterland, OH: Greenleaf Book Company, 2000), pp. 2–3. This book provides effective, practical, step-by-step guidelines to replace the inner effects of stigma with a positive identity. Also, personal interviews.
10. Dweck, Carol. *Self-Theories: Their Role in Motivation, Personality, and Development* (New York: Columbia University Psychology Press, 2000).
11. Dweck, Carol, and Lisa Storich. "Mastery-Oriented Thinking." In Snyder, *Coping*, pp. 233–234 and 249–250. Also see: Niiya, Yu, Jennifer Crocker, and Elizabeth N. Bartmess. "From Vulnerability to Resilience: Learning Orientations Buffer Contingent Self-Esteem from Failure." *Psychological Science*, December, 2004.

12. Ken Cuyler story, personal interviews. Ken was promoted to Commander after outstanding service in Iraq. He is now retired and works as a management consultant.
13. "Stephanie" and "Priscilla" story, personal interviews, names changed on request. Redwood tree cones are serotinous. They open and release their seeds after subjected to extreme heat.

Chapter 7. Unleash Your Curiosity (Level 4)

1. Transistor development history at: www.pbs.org/transistor (accessed September 19, 2004).
2. Freire, Paulo. *The Pedagogy of the Oppressed,* 30th anniversary reissue, Ramos translation (New York: Continuum, 2000), chapter 2.
3. Stacy Scholtz story, personal interviews.
4. Peck, M. Scott. *The Road Less Traveled* (New York: Touchstone reprint, 1998).
5. Somers, Suzanne. *After the Fall: How I Picked Myself Up, Dusted Myself Off, and Started All Over Again* (New York: Crown, 1998), p. 205.
6. Manz, Charles C. *The Power of Failure: 27 Ways to Turn Life's Setbacks Into Success* (San Francisco: Berrett-Koehler, 2002), p. 1.
7. Hyatt, Carole, and Linda Gottlieb. *When Smart People Fail* (New York: Simon and Schuster, 1987), pp. 14, 38, 233.
8. Brodow, Ed. *Beating the Success Trap: Negotiating for the Life You Really Want and the Rewards You Deserve* (New York: HarperResource, 2003), p. 124. Also, personal interviews
9. Esthelle, Betty. "School Child." In *The Best Poems & Poets of 2002* (Owings Mills, MD: Jeffrey Franz, 2003). Reprinted with author's permission.

Chapter 8. Positive Expectations (Level 4)

1. Domino, Brian, and Daniel W. Conoway. "Optimism and Pessimism from a Historical Perspective." *Optimism and Pessimism: Implications for Theory, Research, and Practice,* Edward Chang, ed. (Washington, DC: American Psychological Association, 2004).
2. Emerson, Ralph Waldo. "Self-Reliance." *Selected Writings of Ralph Waldo Emerson* (New York: New American Library, 1965), p. 278.
3. Carver, Charles S., and Michael F. Scheier. "Optimism." In Snyder, *Coping,* p. 182.

4. Wiseman, Richard. *The Luck Factor,* pp. 161–162.

5. "The Difference Between Optimism and Hope." *Newsweek* interview with Jerome Groopman posted at MSNBC website (accessed February 14, 2004).

6. Seligman, Martin E. P. *Learned Optimism* (New York: Simon and Schuster, 1990), p. 30.

7. Peterson, Christopher, and Edward Chang. "Optimism and Flourishing." *Flourishing: Positive Psychology and the Life Well-Lived,* Corey M. Keyes and Jonathan Haidt, eds. (Washington, DC: American Psychological Association, 2003), p. 57.

8. Carver, Charles S., and Michael F. Scheier. "Three Human Strengths." In *A Psychology of Human Strengths,* Lisa G. Aspinwall and Ursula M. Staudinger, eds. (Washington, DC: American Psychological Association, 2003).

9. Mead, George H. "Language and the Development of the Self." In *Mind, Self, and Society,* Charles W. Morris, ed. (Chicago: University of Chicago Press, 1934). This is an excellent early discussion on how the concept of "attitude" evolved from describing animal behavior to describing human behaviors.

10. Stone, Clement. *Success Through Positive Mental Attitude* (New York: Pocket Books, reissued, 1991). This is a classic book on how PMA can change a person's life.

11. Hacker, Stephen K., Marta C. Wilson, and Cindy S. Johnston-Schilling. *Work Miracles: Transform Yourself and Your Organization* (Blacksburg, VA: Insight Press, 1999), p. 48.

12. C. R. Snyder, ed. *Coping,* pp. 9–10.

13. *Fostering Resilience in Response to Terrorism* (Washington DC: American Psychological Association, 2004). A set of fact sheets for psychologists working with adults, children, older adults, first responders, people of color, military families, adults with serious mental illness, and healthcare providers.

14. See the Employee Assistance Society of North America website: www.easna.org

15. Hill, Joanne. *Rainbow Remedies for Life's Stormy Times,* (South Bend, IN: Moorhill Communications, 2002). Summary published with permission. Also, personal interviews.

Chapter 9. Paradoxical Abilities (Level 4)

1. McClelland's report of his predictions of career success with college students can be found in the 1961 television program *The Need to Achieve*, produced by the American Psychological Association for the Public Television series, *Psychology Today*. Old black & white prints still exist in some university audio-visual libraries.
2. Janis, Irving. *Victims of Groupthink* (Boston: Houghton Mifflin, 1972).
3. McClelland, David C., et al. *Motivating Economic Achievement* (New York: The Free Press, 1969). Provides a complete description of the achievement motivation research program in India.
4. Siebert, Al "How to Be Positive About Negative People." *Survivor Personality*, chapter 10, has comprehensive guidelines about this process.
5. The best "type" inventory that allows high counterbalanced scores on all measured dimensions is the revised Singer-Loomis Type Deployment Inventory developed by Larry and Elizabeth Kirkhart. Information available at: www.MovingBoundaries.com
6. Schneirla, T.C. "An Evolutionary and Developmental Theory of Biphasic Process Underlying Approach and Withdrawal." In *Nebraska Symposium on Motivation*, Marshall R. Jones, ed. Vol. 7, 1959. Reprinted in *Selected Writings of T. C. Schneirla* (New York: W. H. Freeman Co., 1972).
7. Maslow, Abraham. *Eupsychian Management*, pp. 20, 88–91.
8. Lee, Bruce. *Striking Thoughts: Bruce Lee's Wisdom for Daily Living* (Boston: Tuttle Publishing, 2000), pp. 32–37.
9. Larry Newman story, personal interviews.
10. Paul Wieand, personal conversations.
11. Thanks to participants at the 2005 Northwest conference of US Forest Service Engineers for teaching me about the coefficient of restitution.

Chapter 10. Synergy (Level 4)

1. Maslow, Abraham. *Eupsychian Management*, pp. 88–107.
2. Csikszentmihalyi, Mihaly. *Finding Flow: The Psychology of Engagement with Everyday Life* (New York: Basic Books, 1997), p. 205. Also see: Csikszentmihalyi, Mihaly, and Jeanne Nakamura. "The Concept of Flow." In *Handbook of Positive Psychology*, C. R. Snyder and Shane J. Lopez. eds. (New York: Oxford University Press, 2002).
3. Bob Foley story, personal interviews.

4. Siebert, Al. "Empathy as A Survival Skill" and "How Handle Yourself With Angry People." *Survivor Personality,* chapters 6 and 11.

5. Agor, Weston H. "How Top Executives Use Their Intuition." *Business Horizons,* Jan/Feb, 1986, pp. 49–50.

6. Day, Laura. *Practical Intuition for Success* (New York: HarperCollins, 1972).

7. Hint: What skill is Socrates known for?

Chapter 11. Serendipity (Level 5)

1. Serendip was the mythical name of the Island of Ceylon, now named Sri Lanka. For an account of Horace Walpole's coining of the word "serendipity," see: Reemer, Theodore G., ed. *Serendipity and the Three Princes: From the Peregriniaggio of 1557* (University of Oklahoma Press, 1965). The original Persian story is in *Peregrination of Three Princes of Serendip,* by Theodore Reemer. (In some libraries the book is listed under the name of the Italian translator, Christopher Aremno.) Careful study reveals that Walpole's childhood memory of an English translation of a German translation of an Italian translation of an old Persian story did not accurately reflect the original. This turned out to be a fortunate (not serendipitous) distortion.

2. Reeder, Jesse. *Black Holes and Energy Pirates: How to Recognize and Release Them* (Freedom, CA: The Crossing Press, 2001). Also, personal interviews.

3. Tom Peterson story, personal interviews.

4. Massie , Lynne. *I'll Be Here Tomorrow: Transforming Tragedy Into Triumph* (Tumwater, WA: Cymitar Press, 2004), pp. 132–133. Also, personal interviews.

5. Marcia Keith story, personal interviews.

6. Paul Wieand story, personal interviews. Website: www.AdvancedEQ.com

Chapter 12. Extreme Challenges (Level 5)

1. Wilkins, Skip, and Joseph Dunn. *The Real Race: The Skip Wilkins' Story* (Wheaton, IL: Tyndale House, 1981). Also, personal interviews.

2. Pflug, Jackie Nink. *Miles to Go Before I Sleep* (Center City, MN: Hazelden, 1995). Also, personal interviews.

3. Cliff Meidl story, 2000 Olympic Games website and online news stories (accessed September 19, 2003).

4. Jozefowski, Joanne. *The Phoenix Phenomenon* (Northvale, NJ: Jason Aronson, Inc., 1999). Summarized with permission.

5. Frankl, Viktor. "Logotherapy in a Nutshell." *Man's Search*, pp. 119–179.

6. Wilson, John P., Zev Harel and Boaz Kahana, eds. *Human Adaptation to Extreme Stress: From Holocaust to Vietnam* (New York: Plenum Press, 1988).

7. Native American untold history from personal interviews, Dr. Tom Ball, and facts presented at "Healing the Wounded Spirit" conferences 2001–2005. For a recounting of atrocities experienced by Native Americans, see: Duran, Bonnie, and Karina Walters. "HIV/AIDS in 'Indian Country': Current Practice, Indigenist Etiology Models and Postcolonial Approaches to Change." *AIDS Education and Prevention*, 2004, No. 3, pp. 187–201. Also see: Walters, K. L., J. M. Simoni and T. Evans-Campbell. "Substance Abuse Among American Indians and Alaska Natives: Incorporating Culture in an 'Indigenous' Stress-Coping Paradigm." *Public Health Reports*, Supplement 1 (2002), 117, No. 4, pp. 520–524.

8. Duran, Eduardo, and Bonnie Duran. *Native American Postcolonial Psychology* (New York: State University of New York Press, 1995), SUNY Series in Transpersonal and Humanistic Psychology.

9. Morris, Debbie. *Forgiving Dead Man Walking* (Grand Rapids, MI: Zondervan Publishing House, 1998).

10. Schemmel, Jerry. *Chosen to Live* (Littleton, CO: Victory Publishing Company, 1996). Also, personal interviews.

11. Elia Zedeño story, personal interviews, and "Falling Together" posted at the www.SurvivorGuidelines.org website. World Trade Center survivors website: www.SeptemberSpace.org.

12. Schnall, Maxine. *What Doesn't Kill You Makes You Stronger: Turning Bad Breaks Into Blessings* (Cambridge, MA: Perseus Publishing, 2002). Also see: Brehony, Kathleen A. *After the Darkest Hour: How Suffering Begins the Journey to Wisdom* (New York: Henry Holt and Company, 1999).

13. Richard Williams and Ken Thompson, personal interviews. Website: www.OklahomaCityNationalMemorial.org

14. Tedeschi, Richard G., Crystal L. Park and Lawrence G. Calhoun, eds. *Positive Changes in the Aftermath of Crises* (Mahwah, NJ: Lawrence Erlbam Associates, 1989). Also see: Updegraff, J. A., and S. E. Taylor. "From Vulnerability to Growth: Positive and Negative Effects of Stressful Life Events." In *Loss and Trauma*, T. H. Harvey and E. Miller, eds. (Philadelphia: Brunner-Routledge, 2000).

15. Bonnano, George A. "Loss, Trauma, and Human Resilience: Have We Underestimated the Human Capacity to Thrive After

Extremely Aversive Events?" *American Psychologist,* January, 2004, pp. 20–28. Additional information about resiliency psychology is available at the American Psychological Association website: www.apaHelpCenter.org

Chapter 13. Transformational Breakthrough (Level 5)

1. I Ching information compiled from interviews with expert practitioners and from these sources: *Understanding the I Ching,* by Cyrille Javary (Boston: Shambhala Publications, 1997). *I Ching: Book of Changes,* translated by James Legge (New York: Bantam Books, 1969). *Eight Lectures on The I Ching,* by Hellmut Wilhelm (Princeton, NJ: Princeton University Press, 1973).
2. *Fragments: The Collected Wisdom of Heraclitus,* trans. Brooks Haxton (New York: Viking Press, 2001).
3. Maslow, Abraham. *Motivation and Personality* (New York: Harper & Bros., 1954).
4. See the movie *What the Bleep Do We Know?* for a fascinating presentation of physicists discussing breakthrough questions about the composition of matter and what we think is reality. Website: www.WhatTheBleep.com
5. See the PBS special *The Elegant Universe* and its associated web page for information on quarks and string theory, narrated and written by Brian Greene: www.pbs.org/wgbh/nova/elegant/ everything.html (accessed January 26, 2005).
6. Fritjof Capra, Fritjof. *The Tao of Physics* (Boston: Shambhala Publications, 1975; updated 4th edition, 2000).
7. Sheldrake, Rupert. *A New Science of Life* (Los Angeles: Tarcher, 1981).
8. Prigogine, Ilya, and Isabelle Stengers. *Order Out of Chaos: Man's New Dialogue With Nature* (New York: Bantam Books, 1984). Also see: Capra, Fritjof. *The Web of Life* (New York: Doubleday/Anchor, 1996), pp. 180–181; Also see: Gunderson, Lance H., and C. S. Holling, eds. *Panarchy: Understanding Transformations in Human and Natural Systems,* (New York: Island Press, 2002).
9. Robinson, Winter. *A Hidden Order: Uncover Your Life's Design* (Boston: Red Wheel, 2004). Also, teleological, here, as defined in the *American Heritage Desk Dictionary* (Houghton Mifflin, 1981): The philosophical doctrine that natural phenomena are not determined by mechanical causes but instead are directed toward a definite end in the overall scheme of nature.

10. Davidson, Richard. "Affective Style, Psychopathology, and Resilience: Brain Mechanisms and Plasticity." *American Psychologist*, November, 2000, pp. 1196–1214.

11. Lifton, Robert J. *The Protean Self: Human Resilience in an Age of Fragmentation* (New York: HarperCollins Basic Books, 1993), pp. 5–9.

12. Strogatz, Steven. *Sync: The Emerging Science of Spontaneous Order* (New York: Hyperion Press, 2003).

13. Wheatley, Margaret. *Leadership and the New Science: Discovering Order in a Chaotic World (Revised)* (San Francisco: Berrett-Koehler, 2001), pp. 75–92. Also see: Robb, Dean. "Building Resilient Organizations." *OD Practitioner*, August 2001. On-line at: www.ResiliencyGroup.com

Index

achievement thinking, 120–123
  counterbalanced traits, 121–137
    and biphasic adjustment, 127–129
    definitions, 122–123, 127–129
    and emotional intelligence, 129–137
    elements of, 121–122
    goal setting, 120–121
    post-traumatic growth (PTG), 189, 198, 199–202
    and self-awareness, 133–134
    and self-esteem, 123–124, 130
adaptability
  necessity for success, 30–32
  and synergy, creating, 144–145
adversity
  "broaden and build," and, 55
  complex systems evolution, and, 198
  decisions, and, 32, 100 (*see also* choice point)
  flow experiences, and, 143
  goal achievement, and, 69 (*see also* problem-solving skills)
  optimism in response to, 110–111, 119 (*see also* optimism)
  and resiliency, essence of, 114
  responsibility, personal, 32–33
  serendipity, and, 158–168 (*see also* serendipity)
  skills, development of, 24–27
  strength, born of, 5, 55, 75
  transformation and, 171–190
agile, 130
agility, 130, 144
Alarm Reaction, 36–37
Angel, Carol, 15–16
anxiety
  learning, experiential and, 103
  self-confidence, and, 76

appreciating pairs. *see also* counter-balanced traits
  and positive/negative thinking, 124–125, 135–137
Armstrong, Lance, 13
attitudes
  change, and
    labels, 126–127
    optimism, 111–114
    positive/negative thinking, 126
authorities
  "good child" and, 9, 10, 192
  questioning, 192
  societal training, and, 21, 76–77
autonomic nervous system. *see also* mind-body connection
  self-esteem, and, 73

barrier paradigms
  "good" child socialization, 9, 10, 39, 192
  locus of control, external, 10, 112–113
  "stress" mythology, 10, 35–52, 192
behavior
  change, and
    learning, through, 103–104
    optimistic attitudes, 111–114
  and cultural restrictions, 95–96
  predetermined
    and problem solving, 96–97
Benson, Herbert, 49
bouncing back
  anxiety, diminishing, 4–5
  barriers to, 2–3 (*see also* barrier paradigms)
  and counterbalanced traits, 130 (*see also* counterbalanced traits)

Acknowledgments

I feel deep appreciation for the hundreds of people whose examples of resiliency helped shape this book. A few are mentioned specifically in the chapters, but for every resiliency story told there are a hundred more without space to include them. For them and everyone who has made a heroic resiliency journey, I wish to express my deepest positive regards.

I wish to also acknowledge the following people:

+ My wife Molly, whose constant love, support, and belief in me and my work is a deep source of strength for me

+ My sister Mary and her husband Chad, who are always available to contribute valuable feedback and professional expertise to my work

+ My niece Kristin, whose amazing talents and years of dedicated work as my office manager, webmaster, IT specialist, book designer, and editor has left me free to do the work I do best

+ Sam Kimball, for years of friendship and valuable editing suggestions

+ Edie Eva Eger, Bernie Siegel, Norman Locke, Bill Harris, Paul Scheele, Phil Evans, deWolff Roberts, Ken Smith, Cindy Schilling-Johnson, Marta Wilson, Sharon Conti, Caryn Tilton, Richard Tedeschi, Stephen Barnes, Larry Kirkhardt, Barbara Clark, Marilyn Trinkle, Jesse Reeder, Dean Robb, Stephen Werbel, Bob Czimbal, Tracy Lenda, Tom and Gloria Peterson, Rob Russell, Jack Kondrasuk, Chuck DeRidder, Stephen Hacker, Tammy Roberts, John Duff, Chris Rush, Glen Fahs, and many other friends and colleagues for their enthusiastic interest and encouragement

+ Stephanie Abarbanel, whose superb talent as a developmental editor transformed a professor's ramblings into a readable book

+ Kimberly Cameron and Elizabeth Lyon, for their warm, encouraging support and marvelous professional skills with authors

+ Gabriele Ganswindt, my other colleagues in the Global Resiliency Network, and the emerging new cohort of resiliency researchers, who are leading the way to a new and better level of human functioning

+ US Forest Service personnel, for their deep commitment to excelling at preserving and maintaining priceless natural resources for future generations

+ Terrorist attack survivors, for their inspiring examples of converting tragedy into a heroic journey of recovery

+ Enos and Charlotte Herkshan and all my Indian nation friends, for their enduring courage and welcoming openness

+ Steve Piersanti and the entire Berrett-Koehler team, for their warm welcome and invitation to participate in their unique vision and mission

+ Public-sector employees, who receive more criticism and less praise than they deserve

About the Author

Al Siebert is Director of The Resiliency Center. He is an ex-paratrooper with a PhD in clinical psychology from the University of Michigan. He is internationally recognized for his research into the inner nature of highly resilient survivors; his book *The Survivor Personality* is published in many languages. Articles by him or quoting his work have appeared in *USA Weekend, Bottom Line/Personal, The New England Financial Journal, Family Circle, Men's Fitness, The Wall Street Journal, The Los Angeles Times, Outdoor Life, Good Housekeeping, CBSHealthwatch.com, Human Resources Magazine,* the *EAP Association Magazine, Prevention,* and *Harvard Business Review.* His popular quiz, "How Resilient Are You?", has been reprinted in many publications. He has been interviewed about highly resilient survivors on National Public Radio, the *NBC Today Show, OPRAH,* and CNN.

Dr. Siebert taught management psychology seminars at Portland State University for over thirty years, was a volunteer recovery group leader with Vietnam veterans for three years, and served as chairman of his county school board.

He speaks about how to thrive under pressure, manage nonstop change, and develop resiliency skills at conferences and meetings of professional associations, public agencies, education and healthcare groups. He also conducts the "Resiliency Advantage" seminar offered by the Eastern Management Development Center.

More information about Al Siebert's resiliency research and a current list of resiliency resources can be found at the Resiliency Center website, **www.ResiliencyCenter.com.**

• • • • • • • • • • • •

Special Note:
The Resiliency Advantage—winner:
2006 Independent Publisher's
Best Self-Help Book Award

Berrett–Koehler
Publishers

Berrett-Koehler is an independent publisher dedicated to an ambitious mission: *Creating a World That Works for All*.

We believe that to truly create a better world, action is needed at all levels—individual, organizational, and societal. At the individual level, our publications help people align their lives with their values and with their aspirations for a better world. At the organizational level, our publications promote progressive leadership and management practices, socially responsible approaches to business, and humane and effective organizations. At the societal level, our publications advance social and economic justice, shared prosperity, sustainability, and new solutions to national and global issues.

A major theme of our publications is "Opening Up New Space." Berrett-Koehler titles challenge conventional thinking, introduce new ideas, and foster positive change. Their common quest is changing the underlying beliefs, mindsets, institutions, and structures that keep generating the same cycles of problems, no matter who our leaders are or what improvement programs we adopt.

We strive to practice what we preach—to operate our publishing company in line with the ideas in our books. At the core of our approach is stewardship, which we define as a deep sense of responsibility to administer the company for the benefit of all of our "stakeholder" groups: authors, customers, employees, investors, service providers, and the communities and environment around us.

We are grateful to the thousands of readers, authors, and other friends of the company who consider themselves to be part of the "BK Community." We hope that you, too, will join us in our mission.

A BK Life Book

This book is part of our BK Life series. BK Life books change people's lives. They help individuals improve their lives in ways that are beneficial for the families, organizations, communities, nations, and world in which they live and work. To find out more, visit **www.bk-life.com**.

Berrett–Koehler
Publishers

A community dedicated to creating
a world that works for all

Visit Our Website: www.bkconnection.com

Read book excerpts, see author videos and Internet movies, read
our authors' blogs, join discussion groups, download book apps, find
out about the BK Affiliate Network, browse subject-area libraries of
books, get special discounts, and more!

Subscribe to Our Free E-Newsletter, the *BK Communiqué*

Be the first to hear about new publications, special discount offers,
exclusive articles, news about bestsellers, and more! Get on the list
for our free e-newsletter by going to **www.bkconnection.com**.

Get Quantity Discounts

Berrett-Koehler books are available at quantity discounts for orders
of ten or more copies. Please call us toll-free at (800) 929-2929 or
email us at bkp.orders@aidcvt.com.

Join the BK Community

BKcommunity.com is a virtual meeting place where people from
around the world can engage with kindred spirits to create a world
that works for all. BKcommunity.com members may create their own
profiles, blog, start and participate in forums and discussion groups,
post photos and videos, answer surveys, announce and register for
upcoming events, and chat with others online in real time. Please join
the conversation!

SUSTAINABLE FORESTRY INITIATIVE   Certified Sourcing
www.sfiprogram.org
Label applies to the text stock   SFI-00341